NORTH
PROVIDENCE

NORTH PROVIDENCE

A History and the People Who Shaped It

Paul F. Caranci

THE
History
PRESS

Published by The History Press
Charleston, SC 29403
www.historypress.net

Cover images: Front: stagecoach leaving Harmony station. *Postcard from author's collection*;
Centredale Hotel in 1873. *Photo reprinted from* The Annals of Centredale *by Frank C. Angell*.
Back: Centredale's business district, circa early 1900s. *Postcard from author's collection*; Frank
Angell, circa 1910. *Photo reprinted from* Looking Backward Four Score Years *by Frank C. Angell*.

First published 2012

Manufactured in the United States

ISBN 978.1.60949.718.7

Library of Congress CIP data applied for.

I have learned much from my family, and I dedicate this book to all of them. My father, Frank, provided a sterling example of the true American work ethic that made this nation great. The example of my mother, Anne, taught me the virtues of love and kindness and the importance of always placing family first in my life. The courage of my wife, best friend and soul mate, Margie, in overcoming life's hardships will always be a source of inspiration. My sister, Linda, provides a prime example of the patience that I so desperately need to learn. My children, Heather and Matthew, whose success in working through and overcoming the occasional "bad hand" dealt to so many of this generation, provide me with hope for the future. Finally, my grandchildren, Matthew Jr., Jacob, Vincent and Casey, provide me new reason for being.

CONTENTS

CONTENTS

ACKNOWLEDGEMENTS

This book would not have been possible without the invaluable assistance of the staffs of the Rhode Island State Archives, the Rhode Island State Library and the Rhode Island Historical Society who provided many images and much information contained herein. Credit should also be given to Frank C. Angell for having the foresight to record much of the early history of the town in two books and to North Providence town historian Thomas E. Greene who has been both an inspiration and an endless source of local historical information about North Providence. Finally, gratitude needs to be expressed for the most generous support of the Antoinette F. Downing Fund for Rhode Island of the National Trust for Historic Preservation. Their funding allowed the Municipal Heritage Group to provide sufficient copies of this book to the North Providence School Department to enable its use as the textbook for the local history education of the town's high school and middle school students.

Part I
INTRODUCTION TO NORTH PROVIDENCE

A BRIEF HISTORY OF NORTH PROVIDENCE

In 1636, Roger Williams fled Massachusetts, eventually settling in Providence with a group of followers. Among them was Thomas Angell, a protégé of Williams's who left England with him in 1631 and followed him to Boston. They settled on land previously purchased by Williams from the Narragansett Indian chiefs Caunaunicus and Meauntonomi. Williams didn't believe that settlers had the right to land simply by moving to it and displacing the natives. Rather, he insisted on purchasing the land from those to whom he felt the land rightfully belonged. The deed pictured here was signed on March 24, 1638, and is the first deed known to exist in Rhode Island.

William's land grant extended from "Fox Point to a bound called the seven-mile line, which is about where the Smithfield Town line is today." As the need and desire for expansion pushed the Providence settlers farther west, a committee was established in 1669 with full authority to sign deeds. With this authority, several territories were established to the west of Providence, and many of these were later granted status as towns. Descendants of Thomas Angell were among those who settled on land later to become known as the town of North Providence. In 1765, many settlers of that land were unhappy with the Providence government since many of its actions tended to favor industrialists rather than the agriculturalists to the west. In response, some 115 petitioners submitted to the General Assembly a request for establishment of a separate township.

The 1638 land grant deed contains the signatures (images) of Indian sachems Caunaunicus (the bow and arrow) and Meauntonomi (the arrow), gra G-Code by Geto Boys nting the land to Roger Williams. *Deed, Roger Williams, copy 1666, C#232, Rhode Island State Archives.*

Though submitted to the assembly in February, action was deferred until the June session. At that time, the assembly granted the request but changed the name of the town from Wanscutt, as desired by the petitioners, to North Providence. There were about 400 free men of the town, of which about 160 resided in the area set off. That area was further reduced on June 29, 1767, when a portion of land was returned to Providence. However, the seat of government was held in the village of Pawtucket, and soon the farmers of Centredale realized that decisions were still being made supportive of the Pawtucket industrialists at the expense of the Centredale farmers. On March 27, 1874, the town was divided again, annexing a portion to Providence and uniting a portion with Pawtucket. It was at this annexation that the land on which the Slater Mill is located—the mill that helped America begin its industrial revolution—was transferred from the village of Pawtucket in the town of North Providence to the city of Pawtucket.

It was also this annexation that transferred the land containing the homes of Admiral Esek Hopkins (97 Admiral Street) and Zachariah Allen (1093 Smith Street) to the city of Providence.

After this division, the present-day boundaries of North Providence were established. Considerable attention was paid to the farming of vegetables and small fruits, as well as the keeping of cows and the sale of milk. In 1870, the population was 20,495, but by 1877, after the divisions, it had shrunk to 1,303. Because of the many rivers that were within its borders, North Providence was a prime location of manufactories. The state established the only Rhode Island powder mill in 1777 on the Centredale/Johnston line. Israel Arnold established a gristmill and sawmill in about 1800. Daniel Lyman opened the first cotton mill in town, the Lyman Mill, in 1809. The Greystone Cotton Mill became operational in 1813, Zachariah Allen established his woolen/cotton mill in 1822 and Richard Anthony and his son built their Greystone Mill (eventually Benn & Company purchased the mill and further developed the mill village) in 1827–28. These mills collectively employed hundreds of people and helped the local economy thrive.

Richard Anthony and his son also established the first store in Centredale in the late 1820s or the early 1830s. James Angell Jr. built the first hotel in Centredale, the Baptists built the first church in 1832 and Edward Capron established the first livery in Centredale in 1833. The town organized its first library with privately raised funds in July 1870 and its first Society (Woonasquatucket Lodge No. 53 of the Independent Order of Good Templars) in 1871. In about 1760, the first schoolhouse was located in Fruit Hill near the Civil War monument. Fruit Hill was well known for its clean air and fruit trees, making this an ideal location. The town's second school was established in 1835 and located at the corner of Smith Street (Old Road) and Fruit Hill Avenue. The school had an excellent academic reputation and became well known. The Fruit Hill Seminary, subsequently called the Fruit Hill Classical Institute, attracted students from the southern states and as far away as the West India Island.

NORTH PROVIDENCE GOVERNMENT LEADERS: THE FIVE MAYORS

In the earliest days of its government, the affairs of North Providence were administered by a part-time council. Over the years, as the need arose, the town created a school committee, a budget commission, a sewer commission and other minor offices. But for the most part, government decisions remained in the hands of the strong council until 1973. In that year, the council adopted a resolution, approved by the General Assembly, creating a new form of government to be administered by a full-time mayor. The new strong mayor/weak council form of government took hold in 1973 with the mayoral election of council president Salvatore Mancini. Mancini had won his council seat in 1964 as part of a reform movement overthrowing the political regime led by Councilman Michael Costello.

From 1964 to 1973, Sal essentially ran the town from his office located on the second floor of the Ace Hardware Store that he owned and operated in Centredale. He governed in the tradition of legendary party bosses who kept a tight control over every aspect of government. He controlled all political patronage and used the Department of Public Works as a favor factory. So, in 1973, when a special election was held to elect the town's first mayor under the newly amended town charter, he was easily elected. He served that office and continued his bosslike control over all government affairs. In 1975, he faced a stiff challenge from District 3 councilman John C. Ricci who, along

This 1987 photograph was taken at a fundraiser for 1988 presidential candidate Michael Dukakis of Massachusetts. Left to right: North Providence mayor Salvatore Mancini, Johnston council president Benjamin Zanni, Governor Dukakis, North Providence council president Peter B. Simone and Johnston mayor Ralph Russo. *Courtesy of Peter B. Simone.*

with others dissatisfied with Mancini's politics, orchestrated a coup to take control of the Democratic Town Committee, the official body able to endorse the Democrat's slate of candidates. The coup, despite successfully replacing Mancini as party chairman, failed to produce a new mayor, as Sal once again easily defeated Ricci in the Democrat primary, as well as the Republican challenger in November 1976. Despite facing serious challenges from G. Richard (Dick) Fossa, councilman at large, in 1980 and 1984 and from District 2 councilman Charles A. Lombardi in 1988 and 1992, Sal retained the office until his death on April 16, 1994.

A. Ralph Mollis was the third elected mayor of the town of North Providence. He went on to become Rhode Island's secretary of state in 2007. *Courtesy of the Secretary of State's Office.*

Council president A. Ralph Mollis assumed the office on an interim basis until an election could be held. During that time, he had to balance a very short campaign window with the duties of the office, which during the months of April and May include preparation and submission of the municipal budget. On August 1, 1994, G. Richard Fossa, a former District 3 and at-large councilman, narrowly defeated Mollis in a five-way race. Fossa took the oath of office as the town's second elected mayor. Fossa was elected to serve only the remainder of Mancini's unfinished four-year term, however, and had to run for reelection in 2005. This time, he was defeated in a rematch with A. Ralph Mollis by only fifty-nine votes in a race that went down to the counting of absentee and shut-in ballots.

With election to the full four-year term, Mollis became the town's third elected mayor. He took office in January 1996 and served until January 2007, when he resigned the position after being elected Rhode Island secretary of state in the election of November 2006. Council president John Sisto assumed the office of mayor on an interim basis and was opposed in a special election by former District 2 councilman Charles A. Lombardi. Lombardi defeated Sisto in the special election, enjoying the support of many of the radio talk show hosts who seemed to resent the fact that Sisto was supported by Mollis and many of the other elected officials in North Providence. Lombardi won reelection to a full four-year term in November 2008 and continues to serve in the position as of this writing.

A ONE-HUNDRED-YEAR HISTORY OF THE NORTH PROVIDENCE TOWN COUNCIL

Many people have served on the North Providence Town Council since the town established its first government. The table in this section traces the makeup of the town council for a period of just over one hundred years.

The longest-serving councilman of record during that time is Oscar Aust, a supermarket owner from the village of Lymansville. He served a total of twenty-four years from 1910 to 1934. Peter B. Simone, who served from 1983 to 2003, is the second-longest-serving councilman, having held the

Peter B. Simone is the second-longest-serving councilman in North Providence. Only Oscar Aust served the town longer. Simone is pictured here with his close friend and political ally, Mayor Sal Mancini. *Courtesy of Peter B. Simone.*

office for a total of twenty years. Rounding out the top five longest-serving councilmen are John A. Celona, who served from 1975 to 1992 (seventeen years); Paul F. Caranci, who took office in August 1994 following a special election and served until January 2011 (sixteen years, five months); and John Sisto Jr., who served from 1989 until he resigned his position to become the interim mayor in January 2006 (fifteen years).

In May 2010, scandal rocked North Providence to its foundation when three councilmen—council president Joseph Burchfield and District 3 councilmen John A. Zambarano and Raymond Douglas—were arrested in the early dawn of May 6 by Federal Bureau of Investigation (FBI) agents in cooperation with the Rhode Island State Police, the Providence Police and the Rhode Island Attorney General's Office following a two-year sting operation. The overall charges included extortion, bribery, gambling, insurance fraud and lying to federal agents. All three resigned their council positions within days, and all eventually pleaded guilty and were sentenced to record terms in federal prison. Eventually, a former town solicitor, a strip club manager acting as a middleman, a former council president, an unlicensed insurance broker and a radio deejay were all charged and sentenced to terms ranging from home confinement to federal prison. All but one pleaded guilty to the charges against them, and that one was found guilty at trial and sentenced to five years in federal prison.

Special elections were held in the summer of 2010 to replace the three councilmen. Alice Brady took office as the at-large councilperson, while Kristen Catanzaro and Dino Autiello claimed the two District 3 seats.

100 Years of the North Providence Town Council

2012–present	August 2010–2011	May–September 2010
		Paul F. Caranci (D)
Stephen Feola (D)	Paul F. Caranci (D)	Mansuet J. Giusti III (D)
Mansuet J. Giusti III (D)	Mansuet J. Giusti III (D)	Joseph Giammarco (D)
John Lynch (D)	Frank A. Manfredi (D)	Frank A. Manfredi (D)
Joseph Giammarco III (D)	Joseph Giammarco (D)	
Alice Brady (D)	Alice Brady (D)	**NOTE**: The council had
Kristen Catanzaro (D)	Kristen Catanzaro (D)	only four members following
Dino Autiello (D)	Dino Autiello (D)	the arrests and resignations
		of Burchfield, Douglas and
		Zambarano.

17

2009–2010	2007–2008	2005–2006
Paul F. Caranci (D)	Paul F. Caranci (D)	Paul F. Caranci (D)
Mansuet J. Giusti III (D)	Mansuet J. Giusti, III (D)	Mansuet J. Giusti III (D)
Frank A. Manfredi (D)	Frank A. Manfredi (D)	Joseph S. Burchfield (D)
Joseph Giammarco III (D)	John Sisto/John Fleming Jr.	John Sisto Jr. (D)
John A. Zambarano (D)	John A. Zambarano (D)	John A. Zambarano (D)
Raymond L. Douglas (D)	Raymond L. Douglas (D)	Eileen M. Cook (D)
Joseph S. Burchfield (D)	Joseph S. Burchfield (D)	Robert A. Ricci (D)

2003–2004	2001–2002	1999–2000
Peter B. Simone (D)	Peter B. Simone (D)	Peter B. Simone (D)
Paul F. Caranci (D)	Paul F. Caranci (D)	Paul F. Caranci (D)
John Sisto Jr. (D)	John Sisto Jr. (D)	John Sisto Jr. (D)
Joseph S. Burchfield (D)	Joseph S. Burchfield (D)	Joseph S. Burchfield (D)
Eileen M. Cook (D)	Eileen M. Cook (D)	Eileen M. Cook (D)
John A. Zambarano (D)	John A. Zambarano (D)	John A. Zambarano (D)
Robert A. Ricci (D)	Robert A. Ricci (D)	Robert A. Ricci (D)

1997–1998	1995–1996	1993–1994
Peter B. Simone (D)	Peter B. Simone (D)	Peter B. Simone (D)
Paul F. Caranci (D)	Paul F. Caranci (D)	Louis Lanni/Paul F. Caranci
John Sisto Jr. (D)	John Sisto Jr. (D)	John Sisto Jr. (D)
Charles A. Lombardi (D)	Charles A. Lombardi (D)	Donald J. Cataldi (D)
Eileen M. Cook (D)	Robert A. Ricci (D)	Robert A. Ricci (D)
John A. Zambarano (D)	Eileen M. Cook (D)	Joseph Cardillo/Eileen Cook
Robert A. Ricci (D)	A. Ralph Mollis (D)	A. Ralph Mollis (D)

1991–1992	1989–1990	1987–1988
Peter B. Simone (D)	Peter B. Simone (D)	Peter B. Simone (D)
Louis A. Lanni Jr. (D)	Louis A. Lanni Jr. (D)	Louis A. Lanni Jr. (Ind.)
John Sisto Jr. (D)	John Sisto Jr. (D)	Charles A. Lombardi (D)
A. Ralph Mollis (D)	A. Ralph Mollis (D)	A. Ralph Mollis (D)
Joseph Cardillo (D)	Robert A. Ricci (D)	Joseph Cardello (D)
Robert A. Ricci (D)	Bruce Iannuccillo (D)	Frank Pontarelli (D)
John A. Celona (D)	John A. Celona (D)	John A. Celona (D)

1985–1986 John W. Rhude (D) Peter B. Simone (D) Charles A. Lombardi (D) Joseph A. Refino (D) Robert A. DiStefano (D) John A. Marino (D) John A. Celona (D)	**1983–1984** John W. Rhude (D) Peter B. Simone (D) Charles A. Lombardi (D) Joseph A. Refino (D) Robert A. DiStefano (D) G. Richard Fossa (D) John A. Celona (D)	**1981–1982** John W. Rhude (D) Joseph E. Rendine (D) Charles A. Lombardi (D) Joseph A. Refino (D) Robert A. DiStefano (D) Ann McQueeney (D) John A. Celona (D)
1979–1980 John W. Rhude (D) Joseph E. Rendine (D) Charles A. Lombardi (D) Joseph A. Refino (D) Robert A. DiStefano (D) Ann McQueeney (D) John A. Celona (D)	**1977–1978** John W. Rhude (D) Joseph E. Rendine (D) John A. Celona (D) Joseph A. Refino (D) Robert A. DiStefano (D) Ann McQueeney (D) G. Richard Fossa (D)	**1975–1976** John W. Rhude (D) Joseph E. Rendine (D) John A. Celona (D) Anthony B. Caranci Jr. (R) John C. Ricci (D) Ann McQueeney (D) G. Richard Fossa (D)
1973–1974 Alfred Gaudet (D) Henry Mazzuchelli (R) Anthony B. Caranci Jr. (R) John C. Ricci (D) Arthur DiSalvo/Tom Zona Sal Mancini/John Rhude G. Richard Fossa (D)	**1971–1972** Salvatore Mancini (D) Alfred Gaudet (D) Anthony B. Caranci Jr. (R) Peter Palmisciano (D) Norman Turner (D) Joseph T. Morrissey (D) John C. Ricci (D)	**1969–1970** Salvatore Mancini (D) Thomas Lund (D) Angelo Iannetta (D) Norman Turner (D) Peter Palmisciano (D) Joseph T. Morrissey (D) John C. Ricci (D)
1967–1968 Salvatore Mancini (D) Thomas Lund (D) Angelo Iannetta (D) Norman Turner (D) John M. Landolfi (D) Joseph T. Morrissey (D) John C. Ricci (D)	**1965–1966** Salvatore Mancini (D) Thomas Lund (D) Michael Costello (D) Benoit Fissette (D) Frank SanAntonio (D) Antonio Ceprano (D) Joseph T. Morrissey (D)	**1963–1964** Walter L. Douglas (D) Thomas Lund (D) Michael Costello (D) Benoit Fissette (D) Frank SanAntonio (D) Antonio Ceprano (D) Joseph T. Morrissey (D)

1961–1962

Walter L. Douglas (D)
Thomas Lund (D)
Michael Costello (D)
Benoit Fissette (D)
Frank SanAntonio (D)
Antonio Ceprano (D)
Joseph T. Morrissey (D)

1959–1960

Walter L. Douglas (D)
Thomas Lund (D)
Michael Costello (D)
Benoit Fissette (D)
Frank SanAntonio (D)
Joseph F. Lynch Jr.
Harry B. Eckloff (D)

1957–1958

Walter L. Douglas (D)
Elmer F. Simpson (D)
Michael Costello (D)
Benoit Fissette (D)
Frank SanAntonio (D)
Joseph F. Lynch Jr. (D)
Harry B. Eckloff (D)

1955–1956

Walter L. Douglas (D)
Elmer F. Simpson (D)
Michael Costello (D)
Benoit Fissette (D)
Frank SanAntonio (D)
Joseph F. Lynch Jr. (D)
Harry B. Eckloff (D)

1953–1954

Walter L. Douglas (D)
Elmer F. Simpson (D)
Michael Costello (D)
Benoit Fisette (D)
Frank SanAntonio (D)
William B. Morrissey (D)
Harry B. Eckloff (D)

1951–1952

Walter L. Douglas (D)
Elmer F. Simpson (D)
Michael Costello (D)
Benoit Fisette (D)
Frank SanAntonio (D)
William Morrissey (D)
Harry B. Eckloff (D)

1949–1950

Walter L. Douglas (D)
Elmer F. Simpson (D)
Michael Costello (D)
Benoit Fisette (D)
Frank SanAntonio (D)
William Morrissey (D)
Harry B. Eckloff (D)

1947–1948

Lynton W. Sweet
Gerald Ponton (R)
John V. Morrissette
Joe Bradley
Michael Fascitelli
Howard J. Merchant (R)
Darwin R. Freda

1945–1946

Stanley F. Cornish (R)
Gerald Ponton (R)
Lyton W. Sweet (R)
Joe Bradley (D)
Michael Fascitelli (R)
Joseph LaCharite (D)
Frank A. Rotondo (R)

1943–1944

Stanley F. Cornish (R)
Leo Desautel (R)
Fred Hardman (R)
Charles Caranci (R)
Michael Fascitelli (R)
Howard J. Merchant (R)
Frank A. Rotondo (R)

1941–1942

Mortimer G. Cummings
Louis Grenier
Russell A. Hebblewaite
James Calderone
James F. McKenna
Howard J. Merchant (R)
Frank A. Rotondo (R)

1939–1940

Mortimer G. Cummings
Frank Sgambato (D)
Ralph Cuculo
Raymond Paquette
Raoul Luminello
Emery Levesque
Edward T. Gilligan

1937–1938	1935–1936	1933–1934
Mortimer G. Cummings	Mortimer G. Cummings	Mortimer G. Cummings
Frank Sgambato	Frank Sgambato	John M. Glenn
Emery Levesque	Emery Levesque	Oscar P. Aust
Philip Russo	Philip Russo	Antonio Zambarano
Ralph Cuculo	Ralph Cuculo	Napoleon J. Trahan
Joseph R. Paquette	Joseph R. Paquette	Ernest C. Adams
Edward T. Galligan	Edward T. Galligan	James E. Pitochelli

1931–1932	1929–1930	1927–1928
William E. White	John M. Glenn	Harry Hartley
John M. Glenn	Antonio Zambarano	John M. Glenn
Oscar P. Aust	Oscar P. Aust	Oscar P. Aust
Antonio Zambarano	William E. White	Antonio Zambarano
Napoleon J. Trahan	John M. Denison	William E. White
Ernest C. Adams	James E. Pitochelli	John W. Denison
James E. Pitochelli	Napoleon J. Trahan	John B. Ponton

1925–1926	1923–1924	1921–1922
Wilman Thornton	Wilman Thornton	Edgar B. Hurdis
John M. Glenn	John M. Glenn	John M. Glenn
Oscar P. Aust	Oscar P. Aust	Oscar P. Aust
Antonio Zambarano	Antonio Zambarano	Robert W. Lister
William E. White	William E. White	Wilman Thornton
Harry Sharp	Harry Sharp	Matthew H.A. Burnside
John B. Ponton	John B. Ponton	Giovani Falco

1919–1920	1917–1918	1915
Edgar B. Hurdis	Edgar B. Hurdis	Edgar B. Hurdis
Oscar Aust	Oscar P. Aust	Fred Swallow
Frank Kelly	Edgar F. Mccullough	Oscar P. Aust
Matthew H. A. Burnside	Wilman Thornton	John T. Northop
Wilman Thornton	Wilman H. Briggs	Wilman Thornton
Euclide P. Payette	Frank Kelly	Wilman H. Briggs
John M. Glenn		Frank Kelly

1913–1914	1912	1911
Edgar B. Hurdis	Edgar B. Hurdis	Edgar B. Hurdis
Fred Swallow	Fred Swallow	Fred Swallow
Robert W. Hay	Oscar P. Aust	Oscar P. Aust
Oscar Aust	John T. Northop	John T. Northrop
Wilman Thornton	Wilman Thornton	Wilman Thornton
John T. Northrop	Robert N. Hay	Thomas Lund
Herbert A. Fenner	George T. Batchelder	George T. Batchelder

1910	1909	NOTE: Beginning in 2002, town councilpersons were elected to four-year terms. From 1910 to 2002, their terms were for two years. Before 1910, all terms were one year in duration. In 1973, the town charter allowed for the election of the town's first mayor.
Arthur Cushing	Edgar B. Hurdis	
Oscar P. Aust	George T. Batchelder	
Harold B. Bullock	Michael J. Kirby	
James Baines	John T. Northrop	
Frank Kelly	George L. Rogers	
George Morrison	Robert W. Hay	
Frank C. Angell	Frank Kelley	

Many of the structures described in this very brief history are still standing. Others, while long since replaced, establish a history that has given us present-day North Providence, complete with its culture, architecture and customs. Using the tour guide located in Part III of this book, take a walk through the several villages of our town and celebrate the fascinating social, religious, residential, commercial, industrial and architectural features of North Providence's past and present.

Part II
BIOGRAPHIES

CAPTAIN STEPHEN OLNEY: HERO OF THE AMERICAN REVOLUTION

Perhaps it was just a coincidence that Stephen Olney would be born in 1756, the very year that George Washington, Olney's future wartime commander, made his first visit to Rhode Island, staying with friends in Newport before continuing his journey to Boston. Perhaps it was divine providence. Maybe it was just an early foreshadowing of things to come. Whichever the case, Stephen Olney arrived in this world on September 17, a fifth-generation descendant of Thomas Olney, one of the first settlers of Providence along with Roger Williams. Stephen's life both began and ended at his family estate on 138 Smithfield Road in North Providence. (North Providence did not become its own town until 1765, so Stephen Olney was actually born in Providence.)

The first nineteen years of Stephen's life were spent in the cultivation of his farm, a pursuit that he enjoyed and intended to make his career. He enjoyed the peacefulness that farming brought him and certainly had all the rural comforts the times had to offer. At the age of twenty, he married Dorcas Smith, a woman three years his senior. Over the years, the couple had a total of eight children, five boys (Joseph, Alfred, George, John and David) and three girls (Candace Mowry, wife of Jabez; Sophia Olney; and Mary King, wife of Josiah). Mary and Josiah King had five children: George, Jackson, Augustus, Sophia and Samuel King. Stephen was most content cultivating his farm, raising his family and otherwise walking in his father's footsteps.

Captain Stephen Olney, hero of the American Revolution. *Courtesy of the Rhode Island Historical Society, RHi X3 9192, Captain Stephen Olney, Rhode Island, n.d., ink on paper PRINT,* Rhode Island Portraits, *vol. 2.*

His only diversion was his membership in the North Providence Rangers, a local patriotic military company organized in the state to enable members to learn military tactics and to be prepared to act in defense of the nation's rights. Stephen could not have known at the time that lessons learned from his passion for farming and family life would soon take a backseat to the military training that the North Providence Rangers had provided him.

Soon after receiving news of the events at Lexington and Concord, events that signaled the start of the American Revolution, Rhode Island organized three regiments to send to battle. Receiving a commission of ensign, Olney was assigned to the company commanded by Captain John Angell. Olney's own trepidation about his military acumen is best described in his own hand:

> *Who recommended me I do not know; but it was not by my own intercession, but perhaps they chose me because they could get no better, so many were deterred from embarking in the cause for fear they might be hanged for*

Biographies

rebels by order of our then gracious Sovereign, George III. I accepted this
commission with much diffidence as to my qualifications; my education
was but common for that day, and worst of all, what I had learned was
mostly wrong...I had no fear that our gracious Sovereign would think me
worth hanging for a rebel.

Ready or not, on May 1, 1775, Olney's regiment received orders from General Nathanael Greene to depart for action. The regiment marched to the North Providence meetinghouse, where they prayed and were blessed. The soldiers embraced their loved ones and friends and prepared for the next day's forty-mile march to Roxbury, Massachusetts.

At the end of the next day, a tired regiment of young boys arrived near Boston to the disheartening sight of a strongly fortified, well-situated band of redcoats. A second band of boys, under the command of Colonel Daniel Hitchcock, made camp on Jamaica Plain and readied for its first taste of combat. That opportunity came on June 17 with the Battle of Bunker Hill. The redcoats heavily bombarded Hitchcock's campsite in an attempt to deflect attention from the goings-on at Bunker Hill. While the number of casualties in the regiment's first combat experience is not clear, the fright was overwhelming, and it was all Captain Angell could do just to keep the boys in rank.

The time between that first bombardment and their evacuation day in March 1776 was an arduous period. The soldiers fought off fatigue, potshot fighting, periods of boredom, frightful epidemics and untold suffering. By the time Washington arrived with reserves, Stephen Olney had distinguished himself for his gallantry and military ability. He was promoted to first lieutenant with the regiment of Colonel Daniel Hitchcock, while Lieutenant Colonel Ezekiel Cornell of Scituate and Major Israel Angell served as his field officers.

By the end of March, the troops were ordered to New York. They made their way on foot via Providence, where Olney was granted the favor of remaining with his family for a one-night leave. Olney missed his wife very much, as prior to his detachment he had never been away from home for more than twenty-four hours at one time. The next day, Olney departed for Long Island, New York, where he and his regiment built fortifications and drove away small bands of enemy marauders that stole whatever they could from the citizenry. Lieutenant Olney helped capture seven or eight of these foragers one night and helped extract important information from them.

In the subsequent Battle of Long Island, and in a clash with British forces at Harlem, Olney was cited for bravery on the battlefield. The battles delayed the regiment in crossing the Delaware River, however, and the men missed the Christmas Day fighting at Trenton. It was just about at this time that the enlistment of Rhode Island's three regiments expired. But at Washington's urging, the entire enlistment stayed on for another month, during which they fought with Washington at the Second Battle of Trenton and helped him score a decisive victory at Princeton. It was in this battle that Stephen Olney would perform the historic deeds that would immortalize him.

Shortly after helping General Washington to victory in a decisive battle at Second Trenton, Stephen Olney's bravery would earn him the honor of being called a hero for the rest of his life. Colonel James Monroe of the Pennsylvania troops was wounded while trying to organize his ranks after being driven back by the enemy. The frightened troops of Pennsylvania were retreating through the ranks of the Rhode Island regiment led by Captain Jeremiah Olney and formed directly behind the Pennsylvania troops. Monroe was able to stop some of them and encourage them back into rank when he was wounded. Stephen Olney ran to the aid of the fallen colonel, dodging fire and bayonets along the way. Olney picked Monroe up, hoisted him over his shoulder, carried him to safety and returned to the battle. Stephen Olney's actions may have altered not only the course of the battle but also the course of America's history. For Colonel James Monroe recovered and went on to become the fifth president of the United States. Stephen Olney never spoke of his heroics except under close questioning, making him a true hero in every sense of the word.

Sometime after this battle, Stephen Olney briefly returned to his home in North Providence for a visit with his family. Here he received the news that he was appointed to the rank of captain. Captain Olney rejoined Washington's army at Peekskill and bravely fought in the Battle of Red Bank. He endured at least part of the freezing winter at Valley Forge, engaged in the Battle of Monmouth and returned to Rhode Island to fight in the battle at Portsmouth.

Olney suffered a wound to his left arm in the Battle of Springfield, and General Washington selected Captain Olney's Rhode Island Company to join the Marquis de Lafayette and lead the charge at Yorktown, where American and French troops had surrounded General Cornwallis and his British army. Captain Olney led his men through the stubborn resistance and received severe bayonet wounds in the battle. Weakened from the loss of blood, he continued to fight and encourage his men, who eventually forced their way through the British ranks, driving them out. Once inside the fort, Olney formed his troops and then fell to the ground, stricken by what appeared to be mortal wounds. He quickly recovered, however, and rejoined his troops within a matter of weeks. Lafayette, after learning of Olney's wounds in the war, was so moved that when the two finally met, Lafayette shed tears of emotion.

In March 1781, Captain Stephen Olney, now a hero of the American Revolution, resigned his commission and returned to his family in North Providence. Stephen Olney's remarkable military career had come to an end, but his service to his state and town had only just begun. Stephen Olney served as a member of the Rhode Island General Assembly for twenty years and as president of the North Providence Town Council for several more. Olney also held a number of other town offices during his life.

His beloved wife, Dorcas Olney, died on December 13, 1813, at the age of sixty. The slightly younger Stephen Olney apparently married again as his will mentions that his wife Elizabeth received the estate that she brought with her to the marriage.

Olney lived long enough to greet his old friend the Marquis de Lafayette when the latter visited America in 1824. Captain Stephen Olney, patriot, war hero, town councilman and state senator, died on November 23, 1832, just after his seventy-seventh birthday. He is buried with his wife, parents and other family members at the Olney Family Cemetery, known as Historical Cemetery NP006, located just behind his estate at 138 Smithfield Road.

Much of the Olney farm was left to the town and is now known as the Captain Stephen Olney Park. The homestead was placed on the National Register of Historic Places on May 1, 1974. The home remained in the Olney family until the 1950s. It is currently under private ownership.

JACOB GOFF: THE RHODE ISLAND POWDER MILL

The American Revolution lasted about nine years if you consider that its first shot was fired with the burning of the *Gaspee* in Warwick, Rhode Island, in 1772 and that it ended with the surrender of General Cornwallis at Yorktown in October 1781. This view may not exactly conform to conventional history, but a good case can be made for its accuracy. Whatever event triggered the beginning of the Revolution, however, does not alter the fact that no Revolutionary War battles were fought in the area of Centredale. Few realize, though, that this village actually made a significant contribution in the colonists' eventual success in that war. For it was the northwest portion of this small village that the Rhode Island General Assembly chose for the site of the colony's only powder mill.

The State of Rhode Island built this house for Jacob Goff and his family as an inducement for him to operate the dangerous Revolutionary powder mill that eventually cost him his life. *Photo reprinted from* The Annals of Centredale *by Frank C. Angell.*

The events that took place during the years 1775 and 1776 caused much anticipation and consternation in men and women throughout New England. Many of the incidents that led to the war for independence had already occurred, and all throughout the colonies, men and women spoke freely of the treacherous times. The people of Centredale and neighboring villages were no different, according to Frank C. Angell, as they "congregated in little groups, earnestly discussing the events that had already transpired, and pledging support to each other, and allegiance to the cause they had espoused." Many hamlets and towns throughout the colony had organized military companies, formed safety committees and collected muskets, swords and other articles of defense. Yet despite the efforts of the colonists, more munitions were needed, and bounties were offered to those who would engage in the manufacture of such items as muskets, cannons, swords, powder and cannonballs. In earlier years, such items were delivered via ship from Groton and New London, Connecticut, but it became so difficult to acquire these items after the fighting began that colonists saw the need to manufacture their own munitions.

In the January session of the General Assembly, a resolution was passed authorizing the payment of thirty pounds to anyone who would erect a powder mill in Rhode Island and manufacture five hundred pounds of gunpowder. To the surprise of the legislators, no one offered his services. In fact, the few men with an expertise in the manufacture of powder knew the life-threatening dangers and economic risks involved in running such an enterprise. The assembly soon realized that its inducement was not sufficient to attract any takers and decided to undertake the enterprise itself. Consequently, in the May 1776 session, the assembly appointed a committee to select a site for the powder mill and authorized £150 to be expended on the land acquisition and mill construction.

After an exhaustive search, the committee selected a site on the banks of the Woonasquatucket River, opposite the sawmill and between the old railroad station and the dam of the former Centredale Worsted Company. (The approximate location can be found today behind and between the Burger King and the Masonic Building just outside Centredale at the North Providence/Johnston town lines.) By mid-June, the mill construction was complete, but still no man came forward to operate it for lack of sufficient knowledge of the gunpowder manufacturing industry.

Hearing of this, the assembly authorized committee member John Waterman to procure a mill operator at whatever price he determined necessary. Armed with imagination and unlimited inducements, Waterman was successful in commissioning an experienced man by the name of Jacob Goff. The assembly, carrying out the offer made by Waterman, authorized an appropriation to purchase land and to build Goff a home to shelter him, his wife and their five children. A suitable home was built about 125 feet west of the bridge crossing the Woonasquatucket (near the present-day North Providence/Johnston town lines).

Goff began operations and soon hired Laban Beverly to assist him. The two successfully manufactured powder from the fall of 1776 to August 1779. Then the unthinkable happened: in late August, the two were asked to remanufacture a quantity of state-owned powder that had been rendered unusable because of the damp conditions in which it was stored. The remanufacturing process was far more dangerous than the creation of the same product because of the volatile nature of the powder, but in a patriotic gesture, Goff and Beverly agreed to take on the task. They engaged in the operation without incident for several days…that is, until the afternoon of August 28, 1779.

On that day, a contaminated mixture on which they worked proved explosive. The ignition of the two tons of finished powder and a sizeable quantity of powder to be refinished caused the sky to glow with red cinder and then haze over with thick smoke. Frank Angell later described the explosion as the "deafening crash of a hundred thunderbolts" and said that the associated shock wave could be felt for many miles. Debris was scattered for blocks, and one of the mill's beams was found nearly three-fourths of a mile away.

The subsequent clearing of the smoke revealed the dreadful sight of a leveled mill. Jacob Goff and Beverly Laban were blown a great distance away and were seriously burned and disfigured. Their suffering would not end until the following day, however, when the soul of each man finally "slipped the surly bonds of earth."

The General Assembly, realizing that Goff died in the service of the colony, offered his destitute family an allowance of $600 for their relief. The powder mill was never rebuilt, and in 1786, the land and Goff's house were sold to Isaac Olney, who built and operated the first gristmill in the area. In the late 1800s, the town's first railroad station—which began operation on August 11, 1873, at 8:00 a.m. when the first passenger train passed through Centredale—was located at this site. Still later, into the 1960s and '70s, All State Lumber, a local lumberyard operated by the Mesollela family, would locate here.

Despite the tragic end to this story, the powder mill built in the village called Centredale successfully produced powder for nearly three crucial years of America's Revolution and, in so doing, allowed North Providence to contribute greatly to the war's successful outcome and the cause of independence.

ESEK HOPKINS: FIRST ADMIRAL OF THE CONTINENTAL NAVY

One of the most significant forces in the American Revolution—the one that prevented enemy escape by sea, a strategy that turned out to be instrumental in the successful outcome of the war effort—was the navy. And when the colonists needed someone to command the fledgling Continental navy, Esek Hopkins rose to the challenge.

Esek Hopkins was born on April 26, 1718, in Chapumiscook, Rhode Island, the area known as modern-day Scituate. He was one of nine children of William (circa 1685–1738) and Ruth Wilkinson Hopkins (circa 1685–1738). His older brother, Stephen, was certainly the more famous of the siblings and a major factor in Esek's eventual appointment as navy commodore. Stephen was a member of the Continental Congress, a signer of the Declaration of Independence and ten times the governor of Rhode Island, serving between 1755 and 1768.

All of Esek's childhood and young adult years were spent on his parents' farm. Shortly after the death of his father in the summer of 1738, twenty-year-old Esek journeyed to Providence to become a sailor. The allure of the sea and the financial rewards that could be had as a privateer were most provocative. Vast fortunes could be made in the colonial days by "pirating British vessels" and taking control of the possessions. The colonists employed this practice at wartime, but many men with an entrepreneurial spirit engaged in the practice for profit, keeping the pirated goods for themselves. In fact, according to notations in Hopkins's papers,

Commodore Esek Hopkins, first admiral of the Continental navy. *Courtesy of the Department of Navy, Naval Historical Center, #.NH 85750-KN.*

held by the Rhode Island Historical Society's Manuscripts Division, this was "Rhode Island's most profitable enterprise during the years before the American Revolutionary War."

Hopkins was a "tall and stout" man of extraordinary good looks who parlayed his strength and work ethic to quickly rise in the ranks of professional seamen. Just three years after leaving home, Esek had become a prominent master mariner. While in port, he met and fell in love with Desire Burroughs (1722–1794), the daughter of Ezekiel Burroughs, a Newport deacon. The young couple married in 1743 and took up residence in her hometown of Newport, where Esek continued his career as a sailor. Together the couple would have a total of eight children.

During the King George's War (1743–48) and the French and Indian War (1754–63), Hopkins applied his sailing experience to become a privateer. His extraordinary success during those years both enhanced his experience as an adept seaman and boosted his purse. Esek was in his forty-fifth year by the conclusion of the colonial wars. Weary from the years at sea, he decided to enter into business with his older brother Stephen. Together they purchased a store in Providence that eventually led to a profitable and, by all accounts, very successful career in a mercantile and shipbuilding trade. It was also around this time that Esek and his family moved from Newport, making their home on what is now 97 Admiral Street in Providence. From 1765 to 1874, however, this area belonged to the town of North Providence, making Esek a resident of that town during the American Revolution and until his death.

Not long after the conclusion of the French and Indian War, there was a growing concern among the colonists that the relationship with the British Crown was deteriorating, making certain the prospects of a revolution. The growing discontent did not escape Hopkins. In fact, by all accounts, Esek was among the rebels who burned the HMS *Gaspee* in Warwick on the night of June 9, 1772, an act that signaled the start of the American Revolution as much as the insurgency at Lexington and Concord did.

As a mariner, Hopkins often sailed for John Brown and his brothers. In fact, Esek captained the Browns' ship, the *Sally*, in the disastrous slave-trading voyage that ended in the death of most of the 140 slaves on board. This relationship certainly may have provided a good reason for Esek to be in Providence that night. Still, there are those who contend that it was unlikely that he was in Providence at the time that the *Gaspee* was attacked. His home, after all, was twenty-five miles away, and there he had eight children to care for. The best evidence of his involvement, however, may have been provided by a *Washington Post* article that appeared on Sunday, April 14, 1907. Though written some 135 years after the incident, the story entitled "Earliest of Sea Fighters: The First Captain Ever Appointed in the US Navy (a Short Biography of Esek Hopkins)" reported, "Certain townsmen of Providence made a daring attack on the British war vessel Gaspee, which vessel had been in the habit of boarding and examining all incoming and outgoing vessels. They caught the Gaspee when she was aground, boarded and fired her. She was burned to the water's edge. Among the boarders were the personal friends of Hopkins, which, fact leaked out afterwards, and it was understood that Hopkins was among them."

As a result of the *Gaspee* affair, the Rhode Island legislature may have been more in tune to the prospects of war than the Continental Congress. Whatever the case, the Rhode Island General Assembly asked Hopkins to serve as the overall commander of the colony's militia, conferring on him the rank of brigadier general in May 1773.

Biographies

When 1775 rolled around, Stephen Hopkins was totally immersed in the Continental Congress's efforts to seek independence. If he hadn't used his clout as a colonial governor to help Esek gain his appointment in Rhode Island, he surely used his position to convince the Congress to "outfit 13 armed vessels and to commission them as the Navy of the united colonies. He also saw to it that Rhode Island received the contract to outfit two of these, and appointed his brother as its commander-in-chief on November 5, 1775."

Esek Hopkins's first assignment was received on January 5, 1776. The order was quite specific:

> *You are instructed with the utmost diligence to proceed with the said fleet to sea and if the winds and weather will possibly admit of it to proceed directly for Chesapeake Bay in Virginia and when nearly arrived there you will send forward a small swift sailing vessel to gain intelligence…if… you find that they are not greatly superior to your own you are immediately to enter the said bay, search out and attack, take or destroy all the naval force of our enemies that you may find there. If you should be so fortunate as to execute this business successfully in Virginia you are then to proceed immediately to the southward and make yourself master of such forces as the enemy may have both in North and South Carolina….Notwithstanding these particular orders, which it is hoped you will be able to execute, if bad winds, or stormy weather, or any other unforeseen accident or disaster disable you so to do, you are then to follow such courses as your best judgment shall suggest to you as most useful to the American Cause and to distress the enemy by all means in your power.*

Yes, one would find this order quite specific in nature. Hopkins, however, did not obey it. Rather, finding a difficult time cutting through the ice on the Chesapeake Bay and into Delaware toward the sea some ninety miles away, he decided instead to sail to the Bahamas. On March 1, he took command of two sloops owned by locals and loyal to the king. Forcing the sloops' crews to guide him to New Providence, Hopkins plotted his raid. Once in Nassau, the small seashore town in New Providence, Hopkins, according to the Department of the Navy's Naval Historical Center records, undertook the first amphibious offensive. On March 3, Hopkins, in a brilliant display of military prowess, landed his marines and sailors. The men seized the local British defensive works, taking munitions desperately needed for the American colonies. On the return to the Block Island channel off Newport, Rhode Island, Hopkins also captured and took command of two British merchantmen and one six-gun schooner. On April 4, Hopkins's fleet encountered and took command of two more British warships: *Hawk*, an armed schooner, and *Bolton*, a bomb brig. From his new prisoners, Hopkins learned that the British had a large fleet off Newport, so he redirected his command to New London, Connecticut.

With the greatest military success of his career now behind him, Hopkins was about to suffer his most humiliating defeat, one that would cut his military service very short. The crew was by now tired and overworked. Those who weren't rendered ineffective from battle fatigue were deemed so from an outbreak of fevers and smallpox. Further, the need to provide crews for the captured ships now sailing with the fleet further reduced their effectiveness. Under these conditions, on the night of April 6, 1776, Hopkins encountered the British sloop *Glasgow* off the coast of Block Island. Despite having seven Continental ships in Hopkins's command (the fleet had been reduced by one due to tangled riggings en route), the *Glasgow*, a twenty-gun frigate under the command of navy captain Tryingham Howe, eluded capture and caused severe damage to the *Cabot*, the *Alfred* and the *Andrew Doria*, three of Hopkins's ships. In addition, ten of his men were killed and fourteen more wounded. Hopkins and his fleet limped to New London, and there unloaded some of the captured tender.

For his actions, Hopkins was praised by John Hancock and defended by John Adams. However, navy opponents both in and out of Congress found opportunity for criticism. Hopkins would also come under intense scrutiny from Congress concerning an issue having nothing to do with this action. For violating orders in sailing to Nassau rather than Virginia and the Carolinas, and for distributing goods taken during the return to Rhode Island without Congressional approval, Hopkins was censured. For failing to sail again and becoming trapped at Providence by the British occupation of Newport in late 1776, Hopkins was unceremoniously dismissed from the navy in January 1778, his command given to his protégé, John Paul Jones.

Hopkins, then age sixty, returned to his farm in North Providence, where he rejoined his wife and their children, now reduced from eight to five due to deaths. Despite his unceremonious discharge from the navy, he remained popular with the people of North Providence. Esek continued to serve his community and state as a member of the Rhode Island General Assembly for much of the next decade before his retirement. He died at home on February 26, 1802, at the age of eighty-two, survived by his wife and four of his children. He is buried with his family at the North Burial Ground not far from his home on land he donated to the cemetery.

Biographies

Esek Hopkins's maiden voyage for the Continental navy provided a clear tactical benefit to the cause of the Revolution. First, he was able to capture and provide to the Continental army a substantial store of artillery and munitions at a time when they were badly needed. The action also served as valuable training for other less experienced naval officers, such as Nicholas Biddle and John Paul Jones. Finally, and equally important to the successful outcome of the war, is the fact that the invasion of the Bahamas disrupted the British effort in the American colonies. Nassau was thought by the British to be much more threatened than the colonies. It was a more important location not only because of its placement in the British trade route but also because of the pivotal role it served in naval conflicts between Britain and France. Throughout the balance of the Revolutionary War, British efforts were frequently deflected from the war in the colonies to their interests away from America. In fact, "English preoccupation with this area would nearly cause her to abandon the war in 1778 and may well have cost her the war in the long run." If this sentiment is true, Hopkins's decision to divert his fleet from Virginia and the Carolinas in favor of the Bahamas not only may have provided for the immediate need of munitions for the colonists but also may have been a major strategic victory.

SAMUEL SLATER: ANOTHER REVOLUTION COMES TO NORTH PROVIDENCE

Samuel Slater was at once known as the "Founder of the American Industrial Revolution," the "Father of American Industry" and "Slater the Traitor." He was dubbed by President Andrew Jackson the "Father of American Manufactures." Just how Slater was considered, however, very much depended on who was doing the considering.

Samuel Slater was born in Belper, Derbyshire, England, on June 9, 1768. He was the fifth son, one of eight children born to relatively poor farming parents. He was forced to work in a local mill at the age of ten to help support his family, but the death of his father in 1782 left the family so destitute that they indentured Samuel as an apprentice to mill owner Jedediah Strutt when the boy was just fourteen. Indentured life was extremely hard, but Strutt treated the boy kindly, teaching young Samuel the practice of cotton spinning so thoroughly that by the age of twenty-one he was completely versed in all aspects of the cotton-spinning industry, as well as the machinery and mill construction.

The Slater Mill was constructed and operated by Samuel Slater along the banks of the Blackstone River in the village of Pawtucket, North Providence, in 1793, some eighty-one years before the incorporation of the separate city of Pawtucket. Slater's genius is responsible for the emergence of America's industrial revolution. *Courtesy of the Rhode Island Archives, Preston Collection, C#858, #252, Slater Mill #4.*

About this time, Samuel learned that Benjamin Franklin, one of the leaders of the American Revolution, and the Pennsylvania Society for the Encouragement of Manufactures and Useful Arts were offering cash prizes for any inventions that improved the textile industry in America. Slater immediately recognized this as an opportunity. Britain at the time had a law against the emigration of textile workers to prevent the passing of information about designs that might be useful to Britain's commercial rivals. So, after memorizing all he could about mill construction, machinery and operations, Samuel disguised himself as a farm laborer and defected to America.

He arrived in New York in 1789, just when the new nation was trying to create its own industries separate from Britain. He immediately began work in a New York textile mill but saw little opportunity for advancement since the mill was having trouble returning a profit. Through a coworker, however, Samuel heard stories about Moses Brown, the Providence abolitionist who had moved to the village of Pawtucket earlier that year in partnership with his son-in-law, William Almy, and his cousin, Smith Brown. Although they tried to operate a mill in the style of Arkwright, they were having great difficulty getting it to work. In a craftily worded letter, Samuel offered his expert knowledge of the Arkwright system that he acquired in England under Strutt, Richard Arkwright's protégé, to help make Brown's mill successful. Moses recognized the asset that such knowledge could convey to his mill operation and responded immediately, writing, "We are destitute of a person acquainted with water frame spinning...If thy present situation does not come up to what thou wishest...come and work [with] ours and have the credit as well as the advantage of perfecting the first watermill in America." This was the opportunity Slater had left England for, and he seized on it.

When Slater arrived in Rhode Island, he immediately noted the antiquity of Brown's machinery and advised Brown to allow him to build a new mill from the ground up, with American design and American-built spinning machines. Brown was convinced by Slater's offer to work for free if he was unable to produce yarn from raw cotton as good as that produced in England. The two struck a deal that provided Slater with the funds he needed to build the water frames and machinery, allowing him to keep half of the profits earned and a half ownership of the capital in the venture known as Almy, Brown and Slater.

Brown arranged for Slater to board with Oziel Wilkinson and his family in the North Providence village of Pawtucket. While staying there, Slater met Hannah Wilkinson, his future wife. Meanwhile, Slater dedicated himself to the construction of the mill, laboring furiously until it became operational. That objective was achieved in December 1790, starting with a workforce of just ten to twelve child laborers. By 1791, Slater was able to add some machinery to the mill operation, but the first few years were primarily spent working out some bugs, trying to acquire good-quality raw cotton and perfecting the performance of the machinery. As a result of these problems, the mill was unable to satisfy customer demand for product. In 1793, with operations running smoothly, the partners decided to expand. They selected a new site along the Blackstone River, constructed a new dam to generate the power to run the mill and built a large mill containing three carders and two spinning frames containing seventy-two spindles. Thus, their first factory, the Old Slater Mill, was opened in North Providence along the banks of the Blackstone River. (At its incorporation as a town in 1765, the North Providence boundary extended all the way to the east bank of the Blackstone River. It remained that way until the annexation of that land to the city of Pawtucket on March 27, 1874.)

Slater's management style was based on a variation of his British experience, one that is referred to as the Rhode Island System and is based on the traditional patterns of family life in New England villages. Slater hired children, ages seven through twelve, to work in his mills and supervised them closely. There is mention of the mill containing "whipping rooms" where children could be disciplined, but it is unlikely that corporal punishment was used. Slater preferred fines to physical punishment. Slater's initial intention was to hire woman and children who lived a great distance from the mill site, but that effort proved unsuccessful due to the close-knit nature of New England families. But Slater, who epitomized the type of out-of-the-box thinking that is so popular in today's business world, resolved the problem by developing the mill village. He brought in entire families by providing mill houses for workers to live, a mill store for them to purchase their necessities and a place of worship for much-needed fellowship.

Before too long, however, disagreement over how best to manage the mill fractured the partnership, and in 1798, the dissention prompted Slater to build his own mill while still maintaining his interest in Almy, Brown and Slater. Slater partnered with his father-in-law, Oziel Wilkinson, in a new enterprise called Samuel Slater and Company. The new partners completed their first mill two years later in 1801. This mill became the first in Massachusetts to employ the Arkwright system. Slater's mill empire continued to grow over the years, expanding his Rhode Island and Massachusetts corporations into Connecticut and New Hampshire. In 1799, Slater entered into another partnership, this one with his brother, John Slater, who left England with an understanding of a new technology employing the "spinning mule." This technology was tried in the "White Mill" headed by John. By 1828, Slater was involved in thirteen different partnerships dealing with manufacturing cotton.

Despite all his successes, Slater's adult life was still a hard one. He lost his true love, Hannah Wilkinson Slater, who died in 1812, leaving Samuel to care for their six young children. Together the couple had already buried four of their children. Still a relatively young man himself, Slater began to suffer the debilitating effects of rheumatic disorder, a consequence of his early exposure in operating his first machinery. His second wife watched over his final moments on earth. Slater's biographer, George Savage White, interviewed Mrs. Slater shortly after Samuel's death and wrote that during her husband's last illness, Mrs. Slater reported that "[h]e bore his various pains and sickness with great patience," recalling that he bade goodbye to her and his children with the final word, "farewell."

At the time of his death, Slater owned thirteen mills and was worth more than $1 million. In addition to his manufacturing leadership, Slater was a philanthropist, the founder of many villages and towns and the person who brought Sunday schools to America. He was only sixty-seven years old when he died at his home in Webster, Massachusetts. His significance to America is exemplified in an honor bestowed on him by President Andrew Jackson and Vice President Andrew Johnson. During a trip to New England to visit some of the cotton manufactories, they learned that illness had confined Slater to his home. Not wanting to leave Rhode Island without meeting the Father of American Manufacturing, the entire presidential entourage traveled to his home to greet him.

Slater's efforts and brilliance launched a new American industry that by the 1815 conclusion of the War of 1812 consisted of 140 cotton mills operating within a thirty-mile radius of Providence, employing twenty-six thousand people who operated 130,000 spindles. While there are those who might consider Samuel Slater a traitor for leaking Britain's industrial secrets to its enemy, he is certainly an American hero who more than anyone was responsible for the emergence of the United States as an industrial world leader.

DANIEL LYMAN: REVOLUTIONIZING THE MANUFACTURE OF COTTON

He wasn't born in Rhode Island, but the lives of people living in North Providence, indeed throughout the entire nation, have benefited from the life's work of Daniel Lyman. Though he has long since passed—and while few alive today even give a thought to the fact that he was ever here at all—the mill and the village he left behind, a village that bears his name, helped shape the town we live in today.

Lyman was born the son of Thomas Lyman in Durham, Connecticut, in 1756. He was commissioned a captain in the Continental army while still enrolled as a student at Yale College and served with distinction in the battles of Ticonderoga, Crown Point and St. Johns. Based on entries from his diary, Daniel Lyman was promoted to the rank of major upon his graduation in 1776 and participated in the Battle of White Plains. From 1778 to the end of the war, he served as both an aide to General William Heath and as adjutant-general of the army's Eastern Department. Because this was an administrative position, there is little written about his participation in the battles of the Revolution or its aftermath except to note that he was the first to greet Comte de Rochambeau and his French troops upon their arrival in Newport on July 11, 1780. This latter fact, however, is evidence of the high

A 1909 photograph showing a portion of the mill developed by retired Supreme Court justice Daniel Lyman in that same year. *Courtesy of the Rhode Island State Archives, 2009–11, Roger Williams Park Museum of Natural History negatives.*

degree of esteem that his peers placed in him. Though Lyman fought in the war for independence, it was not this revolution, but the Industrial Revolution, that would lead him to North Providence and his place in local prominence.

Lyman married Mary "Polly" Wanton of Newport in 1782 and took up residence in the Newport home of her parents. Although a surveyor for the port of Newport, Lyman's chosen profession was the law. He excelled in this area, and in 1802, he was appointed chief justice of the Rhode Island Supreme Court, a position he held for fourteen years.

In 1807, in preparation of his eventual retirement from the bench, Lyman began to purchase several parcels of land, eighty acres in all. He took a county seat in North Providence in 1808, acquired rights to build a dam along the Woonasquatucket River in 1809 and, along with others, incorporated the Lyman Cotton Manufacturing Company on River Road, now called Woonasquatucket Avenue, on July 1, 1809.

Lyman's was the first of many textile mills built along the Woonasquatucket River in North Providence, inspired by Samuel Slater. Slater had established

Biographies

along the North Providence bank of the Blackstone River the mill that helped launch the American Industrial Revolution. Lyman set the stage for the aspiring manufacturers to build several more cotton mills along the Woonasquatucket River in 1812 and 1813.

To provide power to the Lyman Mill, the manufacturers formed a company to build reservoirs upstream to store water for use during the summer's dry months. This experiment proved so successful that it served as a model that was replicated farther down the Woonasquatucket, as well as on industrial rivers throughout America and the world. Lyman's innovations in the use of water led to additional advances in technology, including the Lyman Mill's use of the first water-powered loom used in the manufacture of cotton in 1817.

Transportation to and from work at this time was slow and arduous. The time and inconvenience of the travel necessitated that the millworkers live close to their place of employment. To that end, Lyman developed a small village to house the millworkers and provide for their needs. At the convergence of the two existing mill buildings stands a bell tower that was used to alert workers to the start and end of each workday. While the building is no longer in operation as a mill, the mill complex is still a landmark within the town, situated on Woonasquatucket Avenue at the bend in the road just southeast of the Fogarty Center. The bell is long gone from the tower, but the tower still stands tall as a proud reminder to all of the arduous workday that represented mill life just after the turn of the eighteenth century.

In addition to his many professional accomplishments, Lyman was a remarkable family man, nurturing children and many grandchildren who went on to become politicians and philanthropists. Between 1782 and 1804, Daniel and Mary Lyman had thirteen children. Harriet (1784–1875), the couple's second daughter, married Benjamin Hazard, a prominent Newport lawyer and state legislator, serving from 1809 to 1840. They inherited Polly's childhood home in Newport, which has ever since been known as the Wanton-Lyman-Hazard House. This home, the oldest in Newport, was built in 1697. Once the home of colonial governor Richard Ward (1741), it is located at 17 Broadway in Newport and is currently owned by the Newport Historical Society, which conducts regular tours.

Grandson Daniel Wanton Lyman was born on January 24, 1844, the son of Henry Bull Lyman, fourth son of Daniel and Polly, and Caroline Dyer, daughter of Governor Elisha Dyer. Daniel Wanton Lyman attended Brown University, made his family home in North Providence and parlayed his family inheritance into a small fortune. Then he turned to a life of philanthropy. He died an untimely death at the young age of forty-two. In his will, he left thousands of dollars for charitable causes, including a bequest of $5,000 to the Town of North Providence for a monument to be built at the corner of Olney and Fruit Hill and dedicated to the soldiers of the Civil War. That monument still stands today. On July 9, 2009, North Providence celebrated the bicentennial of the founding of the Lyman Mill in a ceremony that inaugurated a historical walking/driving tour through the various villages of North Providence.

While so many residents of North Providence make their home in Lymansville and thousands of others pass through daily, most are unaware that some two hundred years ago, Daniel Lyman started something that revolutionized the industrial era. He served the town and the state, indeed all of America, with dignity and pride and began a legacy still serving us today.

ZACHARIAH ALLEN: SCIENTIST, INVENTOR, VISIONARY

Zachariah Allen was born to Zachariah and Anne (Crawford) Allen in Providence on September 15, 1795. While little is known of his early years, it is evident by eighteenth-century writings that Allen's childhood was shaped by two tragic events: the pageant of George Washington's funeral and the funeral of his own father, which took place in April 1801, when Zachariah was but five years old. He received his education at Phillips Exeter Academy in New Hampshire and graduated from Brown University in 1813. Although he studied law, medicine and religion, he chose the law as a profession and was admitted to the bar in 1815. He undertook a practice in Providence in the office of the late Senator James Burrill and married Eliza Harriet Arnold two years later. It was said that he had both taste and ability for legal discussions and the discrimination required for a successful practice. For a considerable time, in fact, he seemed wedded to the profession. But he just as quickly grew to dislike the practice of law and turned his attention instead to manufacturing, his family's business.

Being deprived of the genius, enterprise, energy and executive ability of his father didn't alter the fact that young Zachariah carried his father's genes. While engaged in the manufacturing industry, his creativity began to show. In 1821, he constructed the first hot-air furnace for the heating of homes, and in 1833 he patented his best-known device, the automatic cut-off valve for steam engines. But it was in 1822 that Allen would start a project that would leave an indelible imprint on the young town of North Providence and the entire country.

So much more
than a scientist and
manufacturer, Zachariah
Allen was a visionary.
*Courtesy of the Rhode Island
State Archives.*

In that year, Zachariah Allen built a woolen mill on Old River Road (now Woonasquatucket Avenue) along the Woonasquatucket River. In the early days of manufacturing, many mills were lost to fire, but Allen built his mill with various fire safety devices that were considered advanced for the time. The Allendale Mill included stone construction, a sprinkler system, heavy fire doors, a hydrant, a rotary fire pump and a copper-riveted fire hose, the first to be used in American textile mills. In addition, Allen built a heavy firewall separating the picker room, an area filled with highly flammable cotton fibers, from the rest of the mill. Finally, he roofed the structure with slate roof shingles set in mortar.

Having built in all of these fire protection devices, Allen promptly applied for a reduction in his fire insurance premium and was just as quickly turned down. The insurance industry of the early nineteenth century, much as is the case today, depended on the premiums of good risks to subsidize those of poor risks. There was no consideration of loss experience or potential in their determination of premiums.

Allen wasn't about to take no for an answer, as he felt it unfair to impose a socialistic approach to the establishment of insurance premiums. He enlisted the support of other like-minded mill owners in the area to establish a company that would provide insurance to only those manufacturing facilities of the finest construction and the highest degree of maintenance and quality. In 1835, the Manufacturer's Mutual Insurance Company was formed and evaluated each loss with an eye toward reducing future loss potential.

This company, however, lacked sufficient funds to fully insure large companies. So in 1848 Allen established a second company, the Rhode Island Mutual Fire Insurance Company, and two years later, he convinced a group of Boston manufactures to organize the Boston Mutual Insurance Company. Each of these companies followed the principles set forth by Manufacturers Mutual. Eventually, all three of these companies evolved into the Associated Factory Mutual Insurance Companies, aka Factory Mutuals. Once known as the Allendale Insurance Company, the company operates to this day as FM Global, an international company that is headquartered in Johnston, Rhode Island.

Turnpikes began in Rhode Island in the 1790s, and more than a dozen such roads connected Providence to the villages extending to the north and west. Allen had enough foresight to build his mills along the turnpike, making it easy to receive deliveries of raw materials, goods and supplies needed in the manufacturing process. Yet the turnpikes didn't make transportation any easier for the millworkers, who were unable to travel great distances to get to work. A successful mill operation, therefore, required a village to support the workers. To that end, Allen built a mill store, located directly in front of the mill in North Providence. The ground-floor store sold sundries and things that the workers needed to live. The second-floor apartment was leased to the family of James Halsey Angell, the mill's accountant. Frank C. Angell was born here. Allen also constructed several mill houses and a meeting hall that was used both for community meetings and church services. The original plan to locate a library in the basement of that building was abandoned. This church also survives to this day and is called the Allendale Baptist Church.

Allen was obviously prominent in the community and was a member of the Providence Town Council. He helped introduce fire engines to Providence and organized a committee to establish a free library and natural history museum. For all his achievements and successes, however, Allen was forced to file for bankruptcy in 1857, but he continued working in the manufacturing industry by helping manage the Georgia Mills, which his brother purchased, and by helping his son-in-law, William Ely, with the Allendale Mills, which Ely purchased from him.

Zachariah Allen's many accomplishments helped shape Providence and North Providence and had a substantial impact on the state and the nation. But his prominent family also changed Rhode Island forever. Crawford Allen

(1798–1872) was a partner in Philip Allen & Sons, the predecessor to Allen Print Works, from 1830 to 1870. He was also a cotton broker operating as Crawford Allen & Company. Philip Allen (1785–1865), Zachariah's younger brother, served as governor of Rhode Island. Zachariah's sister, Lydia, married Sullivan Dorr. Their son, Thomas Wilson Dorr, in response to the inequities of suffrage that denied a vote to any male who did not own property, led a rebellion in which he eventually set up an alternate government, was elected its governor, was exiled and subsequently imprisoned for treason. The cause for which he ultimately died led to changes in the Rhode Island Constitution that allowed all men to vote regardless of property ownership status. (Women's suffrage had not yet occurred.)

On the night of March 17, 1882, Zachariah Allen attended the Stoddard lecture at Infantry Hall in Providence. He felt so good afterward that he declined a ride home, preferring instead to walk the distance. Once home, he sat at the table with his daughter. It was 11:00 p.m. While engaged in conversation, he put his head in his hands and died suddenly without a struggle. He was in his eighty-seventh year.

Allen's family home at 1093 Smith Street in Providence (formerly part of North Providence) still stands today. It is privately owned and was added to the National Register of Historic Places on September 15, 1994.

RICHARD AND JAMES ANTHONY AND LUTHER CARPENTER: CENTREDALE/GREYSTONE MILL OWNERS AND ENTREPRENEURS

Richard Anthony was born into a relatively prestigious and proud family on the first day of April in 1767. His American lineage can be traced seven generations to John Anthony, who was born in the village of Hampstead, England, in 1607, arrived in this country on April 16, 1634, and eventually settled in Portsmouth, Rhode Island, where he became a free man on July 14, 1640. Richard was the son of Daniel and Mary (Bowen) Anthony of Providence. His father was a surveyor who laid out the Providence turnpike and on whose surveys all the plats of Providence are founded.

Richard's brother, William, younger by eight and a half years, fathered perhaps the most celebrated of all the Anthonys, as his fourth child, Henry Bowen Anthony, eventually became an editor and owner of the *Providence Journal* in 1840, governor of Rhode Island in 1849 and, ultimately, a United States senator, taking his seat in Washington, D.C., in March 1859. He

The Centredale Mill as it looked in 1875. *Photo reprinted from* The Annals of Centredale *by Frank C. Angell.*

served until his death on September 2, 1884. But while Henry Bowen is the most notable member of the Anthony family, it was Richard and his son, James, who had the greatest impact on the town of North Providence.

Richard entered the manufacturing business at a relatively young age and, in association with his brother, William, became a pioneer in the manufacture of cotton in Coventry, Rhode Island. On May 12, 1801, Richard married Abigail Eddy, the daughter of Captain Barnard and Patience Eddy. Her father was a naval captain in the Revolutionary War and a descendant of Samuel Eddy the Pilgrim. The couple had a total of eight children, including son James, who was born on September 17, 1795. After many successful years of business with his brother, Richard moved to North Providence, where he purchased the Greystone Cotton Mill in 1816. At the time, the Greystone Mill was relatively small, as it had just been built in 1813. He did not expand its operations and did not do much by way of creating a village there. He sold his interest in the mill to Joseph Westcott in 1835. It wasn't until Joseph Benn and Company purchased the mill in 1904 that the village sprang to life, with mill houses, a social club and the Whitehall building that housed an auditorium, shops and housing units for mill overseers.

In 1823, Richard purchased a half interest in the Centre Mill in Centredale from Israel Arnold. Just three years later, his son James purchased the other half interest, and together Richard and James operated the mill under the name Richard Anthony & Son.

A few years earlier, on June 22, 1818, James Anthony had married Sarah Porter Williams, of Brimfield, Massachusetts, and together the couple had nine children. Mrs. Anthony descended from a long line of Congregational ministers, including the president of Yale and the founder of Williams College. The most prominent ancestors were Reverend John Williams, the renowned "Redeemed Captive" of history, and William Williams, one of the signers of the Declaration of Independence.

At the time of his purchase, the Centre Mill had only twelve operating cotton looms. Taking advantage of Richard's plethora of experience in the manufacture of cotton, the Anthonys made several improvements to the building, including the construction of a forty- by eighty-foot addition that allowed for expansion of the operation to fifty looms. They sold their product in New York and Philadelphia and established a very successful business. The wooden weave room from the original mill was moved across the street and converted into a four-tenement house, the start of a new mill village in Centredale.

To complete development of the mill village, the Anthonys built several more mill houses along Waterman Avenue and a factory store located at the corner of Smith Street and Waterman Avenue, today the location of Sak's Centredale Liquors. The factory store, the first in Centredale, opened sometime in the mid-1820s and provided a place where millworkers and other village dwellers could purchase all the goods and supplies needed for their sustenance. Nineteenth-century millworkers were expected to work an arduous day that often started at 4:30 a.m. and didn't end until 8:00 p.m. They were given only thirty minutes for each of their three meals and, as a consequence, had no time to travel to Providence to shop for their necessities. Workers were paid infrequently in those days, and although they expected to be paid at the end of each month, they sometimes had to wait an entire year for their money. By that time, the balance owed to the factory store consumed most of their wages. This is not to imply that the Anthonys were overly demanding of, or excessively unfair to, their employees. It is just the way mill life was in the nineteenth century.

By 1830, Centredale was beginning to grow in population and had more than doubled in size thanks in large part to the presence of the mill. In addition to several other houses, the village had the variety store, a blacksmith, a wheelwright and a tavern. Demand now existed for a place of worship, and the Anthonys stepped up to the plate. Richard and James helped secure a substantial sum of money that was used to construct a Free Will Baptist Church on Smith Street where Our Place now stands. The stone structure was thirty-seven by fifty-six feet, had a square belfry on the front and was built on land secured from James Angell. With the completion of construction in 1932, attention turned to the procurement of the bell to hang in the belfry. Again, James Anthony was a prime mover. He donated fifteen dollars of the ninety-eight dollars needed to purchase a six-hundred-pound bell made of Spanish bell metal and inscribed it with words that were forever lost when the church building and all its records were destroyed by fire in 1892.

A short time after the Anthonys started the store in the mid-1820s, an enterprising young man by the name of Luther Carpenter took up employment there. Luther was indefatigable and paid strict attention to business. Despite being a man of only "fair education," Carpenter could drive a shrewd bargain. He was incredibly tactful and employed sound business practices. Frank C. Angell described him as "one of the most successful men, from a business standpoint, that Centredale has had."

Luther eventually married Mary Elizabeth, the sixth child of James Anthony. Shortly thereafter, the store was turned over to Luther's care. Under his management, business increased dramatically, and it became obvious that

Luther Carpenter was highly respected for his management skills. After successfully clerking at Centredale's first mill store at the junction of Smith and Waterman for many years, Luther married the mill owner's daughter, Mary, and eventually became the store's owner. Under his management, the store grew so successful that more room was needed, prompting the construction of a new, larger building. This is the Carpenter home on Smith Street in the heart of Centredale's business district. *Postcard from the collection of Dan Brown.*

the one-story building would no longer suffice. Luther purchased a lot at the corner of Smith and Mineral Spring Avenue and erected a new building in 1847. After moving the contents to the new location, he very quickly created a model store from which he hung a hand-painted sign that read simply "Country & Variety Store." From 1858 to 1883, the post office operated out of Carpenter's store, and Luther served as assistant postmaster, a position he finally relinquished at the age of eighty-three when his employee, George T. Batchelder, was appointed postmaster. Carpenter continued as one of Centredale's most successful businessmen until his death, which came suddenly on October 7, 1886. The eighty-six-year-old Carpenter, who had rarely suffered a sick day in his life, died of a heart attack, leaving behind an incredible legacy of success.

James Anthony preceded Luther, passing away in 1836 at the young age of forty-one. Sixty-nine-year-old Richard was in declining health himself and had relied heavily on the exceptional business acumen of his son in the administration of their affairs. With James gone, Richard decided to retire and sold the very profitable Centre Mill to Joseph Cuniff in 1838. Although Richard Anthony eventually succumbed to his afflictions, the effects of his entrepreneurial spirit, many accomplishments and civic participation left an indelible mark on a small, growing village that survives to this day.

JAMES ANGELL JR. AND JAMES HALSEY ANGELL: THE EMERGENCE OF THE CENTREDALE BUSINESS DISTRICT

Without question, the Angell family was the most influential in making the village of Centredale not only the center of commerce in North Providence but the seat of the town's government as well. Their heritage dates to Thomas Angell, who left England in 1631, accompanied Roger Williams to Providence in 1636, serving as his protégé, and spawned the subsequent generations that acquired, divided and developed his land to the north of Providence along the Woonasquatucket River. This is the land that Thomas Angell acquired as part of the original purchase from Narragansett Indian sachems Meauntonomi and Caunaunicus—the area now known as North Providence.

In *The Annals of Centredale*, Frank C. Angell delineated the line of ancestry from Thomas through himself as follows: "Thomas Angell and his son John; his son John Jr.; his son Stephen; his son James; his son James Jr.; his son James Halsey and his son Frank C. Angell." This makes James Angell Jr. the

James Angell Jr., a fifth-generation lineal descendant of Thomas Angell (who accompanied Roger Williams to Providence), was born in 1781. He was described as a tireless worker who never suffered from sickness until the illness that took his life at the age of eighty-nine. *Photo reprinted from* The Annals of Centredale *by Frank C. Angell.*

James Halsey Angell worked as an accountant for Zachariah Allen and clerked in Allen's Mill Store part time while residing with his wife and children on the building's second floor. *Photo reprinted from* The Annals of Centredale *by Frank C. Angell.*

great-great-great-grandson of Thomas Angell and James Halsey Angell the great-great-great-great grandson.

James Angell Jr. was born on December 5, 1781, the son of James Angell and Amey Day, daughter of Nathaniel Day. Said to be of a strong, robust constitution, James Jr. was raised on his father's farm and never fatigued or got tired of his work. He and his brother Nathaniel served as apprentices to their brother Emor, an expert carpenter, and from him they learned the trade. James purchased a portion of his father's homestead from his brother Nathaniel and continued to improve the property his entire life. He married Lydia Olney and had six children with her. He later married Selinda Ray and had two additional children, including James Halsey Angell, who was born on May 10, 1822.

After a period of immigration to New York (1808–1811), the "far west" as it was then called, James Angell Jr. returned to North Providence and leased a farm and tavern on the corner of Fruit Hill and Smith Street (the current site of the Fruit Hill Apartments) that he renamed the Fruit Hill Tavern. When the lease expired in 1822, James decided to build a new tavern in the village of Centredale. In 1824, after almost two years of construction, a beautiful thirty- by fifty-five-foot two-story house was erected on the site where Capital Billiards now stands. The structure had ten fireplaces, two brick ovens, a banquet hall with an orchestra balcony

The Centredale Hotel was established in 1824 by James Angell. It soon became one of the most popular and hospitable taverns in the northern part of the state. *Photo reprinted from* The Annals of Centredale *by Frank C. Angell.*

and a very attractive tavern room, with benches and oak chairs surrounding an open fireplace. The four-foot-high bar was quite modern, with artistic woodcarvings and massive mirrors. Although the sign hanging outside read "Center Hotell—J.A. Angell," the establishment would always be known as the Center Tavern and would "soon became the most popular and hospitable tavern in the northern part of the State." Travel from Smithfield and points north to the city of Providence took two days in 1824, and the Center Tavern is where most travelers spent the evening, at a rate as low as twenty-nine cents per night. Brandy and rum could be purchased for four cents a glass, while whiskey and gin cost three cents. Cigars could be purchased for one cent each or six for five cents.

James Jr. possessed "a genial and pleasant disposition," was courteous to everyone he met and "seemed to possess a certain amount of unassumed dignity which commanded a respectful recognition from all." With these qualities driving his business acumen, he successfully operated the Center Tavern for seventeen years until 1841, when his son, Nathaniel, took over its administration.

James Jr. took an active part in all of the moral and intellectual affairs of the town and held many town offices, including that of state representative in the General Assembly, a position he filled from 1843 to 1845. He and his second wife, Selinda, are buried at Historical Cemetery No. 3 at the corner of Sweet and Walter Streets in Centredale.

James Halsey Angell, known as Halsey, received a "good common school education" and early in life began to work for Zachariah Allen as both an accountant in the Allendale Mill and as a clerk in the mill store. In 1842, at the age of twenty, he married Sarah Angell Capron, daughter of Edwin and Deborah (Angell) Capron. He purchased the store from Allen and operated it while taking up residence on the second floor. There his wife gave birth to their two sons, George F. and Frank C. Angell, the latter being born in 1845. While earning a fair living, Halsey decided to sell the store in 1846, and in November 1847, he took over the management of the Center Tavern, succeeding his brother Nathaniel. He moved to his father's farm in Centredale and successfully operated the hotel and tavern until April 1, 1858, thus keeping management of the tavern in the Angell family for almost thirty years.

In 1854, Halsey was appointed postmaster at Centredale and held that office for many years. For thirty-three years, Halsey kept a daily diary of things that happened in town. He never missed a day's entry, and his journal was so accurate that neighbors often consulted his writings to settle disputes.

In 1863, as the Civil War raged on throughout America, Halsey Angell purchased the Free Will Baptist Church building, built circa 1832 on the site of the present-day Our Place, and converted it to Armory Hall. It was used as both a drill/training hall for Civil War soldiers and an entertainment center, hosting several theatrical performances until it burned down in 1892. On September 5, 1868, Halsey was made a member of the Temple Lodge No. 18 of the Greenville Masons, something to which he had long aspired.

His father, James, who had never before suffered from illness, died in 1870 at the age of eighty-nine, leaving his entire estate to Halsey. At that point, James Angell's estate constituted most of what is now known as the business district of Centredale.

In 1876, Halsey became a charter member of the Roger Williams Lodge No. 32, AF&AM, a chapter of the Masonic Temple that he and his son, Frank, helped organize. Their meetings were held on the second floor of Armory Hall. Although Frank was the prime mover, Halsey also helped organize the Union Free Library in North Providence and served as its treasurer until his death fifteen years later.

In 1889, James Halsey Angell was stricken with paralysis. He suffered with this infliction until July 1, 1890, when, in his sixty-ninth year of life, he quietly died. So respected was he in Centredale that all places of business were closed for his funeral, at which he received full Masonic honors. He is buried in a family plot in Providence at the North Burial Grounds. At the time of his death, the boundaries of North Providence extended that far to the northeast.

Today, while many residents may not recall the lives and early contributions of James Jr. and James Halsey to the village they call home, they might unwittingly pay tribute to Centredale's early entrepreneurs and societal leaders each time they gaze up at street signs that bear their names, Angell Avenue and Halsey Street.

THE STORY OF FRANK CAPRON ANGELL

There isn't much in Centredale that was developed without the hand of Frank C. Angell. We know this because he told us so. In his two books, *The Annals of Centredale* (1909) and *Looking Backward Four Score Years* (1925), Angell chronicles both the history of Centredale and his own life.

It may have been a coincidence that Frank Angell was born in a building owned by someone of the stature of Zachariah Allen, or perhaps it was a

Frank C. Angell never married but always had time for children. He was a wealthy businessman and philanthropist who was responsible for many of the social happenings of his day. His legacy lives on today in the library, the town hall, the Masonic Hall, the World War I statue in Centredale and in many other historic landmarks. *Photo reprinted from* The Annals of Centredale *by Frank C. Angell.*

foreshadowing of what the child's life was to become. Either way, it was probably impossible to imagine on March 9, 1845, as Sarah Capron Angell labored in the second-floor apartment above the Allendale Mill store, that her second son would become the most prominent of Centredale's "royal" family.

Frank's father, James Halsey, sold the mill store and moved to Centredale to run the hotel owned by his father, James Jr., when Frank was just three years old. As a youngster, he was somewhat spoiled by his father's wealth. An animal lover, he kept many dogs, cats, pigeons, guinea pigs, rabbits and a prized gray African parrot. Frank would sit for hours with his mother, father and older brother, George, and sing songs. His father had a voice that would rival the professionals, and George inherited his talent. Frank couldn't sing a note but did learn to play several instruments and helped provide the family entertainment. This experience would one day lead Frank to become a major factor in starting a town band.

Frank was also a mischievous boy. He recounts the day when he was walking with his brother, George, and some friends past the old schoolhouse that had just been abandoned in favor of a new, larger one. Frank threw a stone in its direction and accidentally broke a window. Enjoying the laughter of the others, Frank threw another stone and then another. He eventually broke every window on one side of the building and some on the other side. In typical fashion, however, his father came to his aid in settling the account. Ever the businessman, his father found that it was more economical to buy the building than to pay for the damage. So he purchased the old schoolhouse, moved it to another lot and converted it to a tenement house.

Although mischievous, Frank was exceptionally honest, something of a rarity in young children. One day, he was caught breaking the school's golden "no talking" rule. When questioned by his teacher, he denied it and seemingly got away with it. Frank, however, lost his battle of conscience and the very next day imposed his own after-school punishment. When asked by the teacher why he remained after the bell, young Frank burst into tears and confessed his transgression. He was quickly forgiven by his teacher and released, but it was some time before Frank was able to forgive himself.

Even the most spoiled of children mature, and Frank was no exception. At the age of sixteen, Angell began work as an apprentice harness maker at the village livery stable, earning a weekly salary of $3.50. He remained employed there for some twelve years, and at about the age of thirty, he opened his own livery business, which he successfully managed for many years. He became quite accomplished and in 1874 competed in the State Fair held by the Agricultural Society. His efforts earned him a medal and $20.00. Later that year, he also won at the Woonsocket Fair. In 1892, he retired from the harness-making business to pursue a career in real estate.

Frank was an avid reader and collector of books, two qualities that led him, at the ripe old age of twenty-three, to become a prime mover in the development of a free library in the town. To raise the funds necessary to start the library, Angell held a series of theatrical productions that were staged in the Armory Hall. The first, *All Is Not Gold That Glitters*, was held on Saturday evening, October 31, 1868. Frank not only produced and directed many of the productions but also starred in the leading role. Involving his entire family and many community members, enough money was raised to buy land, erect and furnish a building and purchase 350 volumes. The building, located on the vacant lot to the left of the modern Elliott Robbins Funeral Home, was opened on July 4, 1870. Angell was named the first librarian and served until his death in 1928. Centredale residents no longer had to take the long round-trip carriage ride to Providence to check out a library book.

Not all of Angell's time was consumed with work. In 1888, the photography "fad" had hit, and curiosity led him to purchase a camera and not just take photographs but also develop, plate, print and mount them. As an amateur, Frank photographed everything and everyone he saw. Before long, friends and strangers alike would ask for his services. The strangest request he received was from parents whose twelve-year-old son had died of scarlet fever during the outbreak that hit the village. They wanted a portrait to remember their son by. Fearing infection, Frank refused. The desperate parents suggested propping the dead boy up in a window, enabling Frank to photograph him from the outdoors, but without proper lighting and still fearing contagion, Angell steadfastly refused. In 1890, Frank entered the State Fair at the Narragansett Trotting Park and won first place for his photographic works. This was only the first of many first-place awards he would receive for his photographic entries.

Frank Angell was developing a reputation of being both accomplished and successful. He was becoming a community leader, and his work would soon change the face of Centredale. He had established himself as a leader early in his life. A hard worker, Angell realized success in everything he did. As a hired hand in the village's first livery stable, as an entrepreneur in his own livery business, as a real estate investor and as an amateur photographer, Frank Angell was a winner.

As were many residents of Centredale, Frank and his dad were Masons. Participation, however, required traveling significant distances, as there was no lodge near the village. On September 15, 1875, several local Masons met to consider forming a new lodge. James Angell was asked to preside, and Frank was chosen as secretary. Twenty-six Masons signed a petition asking the grand master of the Rhode Island State Lodge for permission to open Roger Williams Lodge No. 32, AF&AM. Permission was granted, and the first meeting of the new lodge took place at the Railroad Hall building on March 4, 1876. Frank was formally elected secretary and served almost until his death.

In 1884, when Frank Angell was still only thirty-nine years old, he and his friend George A. Cozzens taught seven other friends to play instruments, and together they started the Young American Fife & Drum Band, which soon became the best-known and most popular band of its kind in Rhode Island. Frank played both the fife and the flute. Before long, the band had expanded to twenty-four pieces as other young adults from the village sought to join. They purchased uniforms with money earned through a series of entertainments in which the band members starred. They wrote their own productions to save money, and Frank always served as stage manager. He painted the scenery, made all stage props and trick furniture and provided all the costumes. Both the band and the entertainments served to increase community pride, something that Frank was always a prominent part of.

As he began to mature, Angell became involved in the political affairs of the day. His political leanings were Republican, and at the age of forty,

Biographies

Angell was appointed town treasurer in February 1885 to complete the unexpired term of William H. Angell. In June of that year, he won election to the position in his own right and served until 1897. He was also elected to the town council and served for a number of years in the state's General Assembly. There he served on several committees essential to the town's future, including one to bring a railroad to Centredale and another to bring in water service from Providence. He also helped shape the modern education system.

Angell was a devout Protestant Episcopalian. Yet there was no place of worship in town. About the time of Frank's birth, in 1845, occasional services were held in the Centredale Baptist Meetinghouse (today the site of Our Place), a building that was later converted to Armory Hall and used to train Civil War recruits after Frank's father purchased it in 1863. But it wasn't until a few years after the building was destroyed by fire in 1892 that Frank decided to donate prime land at the intersection of Woonasquatucket Avenue and Smith Street, where St. Alban's Episcopal Church is now located. In 1899, Angell chaired a building committee that selected the architects and carpenters to construct the church. Angell remained active as both a benefactor and a churchwarden until his death.

Frank Angell was first with an idea to improve the village, first to volunteer in its service and first to reach into his own pocket to provide funding. It should be of no surprise, then, that in 1904 it was Frank Angell who purchased the first automobile in Centredale, a Ford Model T. It was also Frank who stepped up to provide enjoyment and entertainment for the children. Every Fourth of July, Angell purchased fireworks for the children to light. It was this generosity in 1904 that nearly cost him his life. On one night of the Fourth, "someone carelessly fired a cannon cracker, a large fire cracker, and a portion of the barrel tube hit Frank square in the right eye." He was knocked unconscious and carried to his home, where a doctor said the blow could have been fatal. Although he survived, the sight in his right eye was completely destroyed.

Despite the loss of his right eye, Frank's patriotism never wavered. In 1919, his seventy-fourth year, Frank served as treasurer on a committee to erect a World War I monument to honor the town's veterans. The committee chose John G. Hardy to sculpt a statue, and Frank personally searched for the appropriate stone on which to erect it. The Gorham Company cast a bronze statue, and a war cannon was secured to place in front of the monument. On May 20, 1920, many townspeople turned out for a dedication ceremony for Centredale's only war monument. The monument still stands today in front of St. Alban's

The Annals of Centerdale

IN THE TOWN OF

North Providence, Rhode Island

Its Past and Present

1636 1909

The Village of Centerdale

BY

FRANK C. ANGELL

An interesting and historic account of an OLD TIME NEW
ENGLAND VILLAGE, from its first settlement to the present
time.
The book has 212 pages and 32 illustrations and two original
maps—is printed upon heavy coated paper, bound in full cloth
with gold stamp.

For Sale by all Leading Book Stores and by

FRANK C. ANGELL

CENTERDALE, R I

Price   -   -   - $2.50

Frank C. Angell is the single person most responsible for chronicling the early history of the village of Centredale. He wrote two volumes, the second being published in 1925, just three years before his death. This full-page promotional ad was placed in the 1910 edition of the North Providence–Johnston Directory.

Church at the point of Smith Street and Woonasquatucket Avenue, although the cannon was taken away when the Centredale bypass was added in the 1970s. The cannon's current whereabouts are unknown.

Frank Angell's life certainly had a profound impact on North Providence and particularly on the village of Centredale. His generosity and impact, however, didn't end with his death on December 12, 1928. He left enough money to the Masonic Lodge that it was able to build a new Masonic Hall. In 1929, the cornerstone was laid at 2121 Smith Street, and the building has long outlived the lodge itself. Frank also bequeathed to the town the land on which his own home rested on the condition that the land would be used to build a new town hall that would bear his name. At a financial town meeting in 1929, the voters accepted the gift and authorized the town council to sell a bond issue of $50,000 to proceed with the construction of the town hall. His Victorian home was sold and moved to 20 Sweet Street, where it still stands today. The large barn in Frank's backyard was purchased by Harry Sharpe, moved to 2251 Mineral Spring Avenue and converted to the Sharpe family home. Harry's daughter, Elsie, married undertaker Elliott Robbins, and the couple received the home as their wedding gift. Today, though extended many times, the original barn roofline can be seen within the construction of the Elliott Robbins Funeral Home. Ground for the new town hall was broken on November 3, 1930, and on June 15, 1931, the Frank C. Angell Memorial Town Hall was completed. The building, enlarged in 1979 to accommodate a growing bureaucracy, remains the seat of government to this day.

SENATOR FRANK SGAMBATO: MAN OF THE PEOPLE

As the twentieth century unfolded, ethnic immigration began to affect many aspects of North Providence. The English/Yankee influence of Stephen Olney, James Angell James Halsey Angell, Frank Angell, Daniel Lyman, Zachariah Allen, Richard Anthony and his son, James Anthony, was soon overtaken, first by the French and eventually by the wave of Italian immigrants who settled in the town. Not unlike that of the English, the work ethic of these immigrants was admirable, and it wasn't long before their leadership abilities became prominent. One such person with political leadership qualities who had an extraordinary influence on the residents of North Providence, and all of Rhode Island, was Frank Sgambato.

Sgambato was born to Giovanni and Carmella (DeLucia) Sgambato in New York City on August 24, 1900. There Giovanni, who operated a local Italian grocery store, imparted to young Frank the virtues of an honest, hard day's work. When Frank was only fourteen, his family moved to North Providence, and Frank took employment at the local textile mills. In those days, it was not

Senator Frank Sgambato was a powerful local official who worked tirelessly on behalf of safe working conditions for millworkers and other laborers in Rhode Island. *Courtesy of Jeffrey Gibbons.*

uncommon for a textile worker to labor in many mills, walking from one to the other, depending on which might have work available at the time. The work conditions in the local mills were difficult for anyone, but they were particularly arduous for a twelve-year-old who would often be required to begin the workday at 4:30 a.m. and continue until 8:00 p.m., with only a half-hour break at meal time. But this experience was the impetus that launched the vision of what would become Frank's life's passion.

In 1920, Frank joined the U.S. Navy, in which he served for two years and was a member of the navy band. His military service reinforced his disciplined work ethic and further shaped the leadership qualities that would soon become an evident part of his being.

Once back in North Providence, Frank continued to work in a variety of factories—cotton, woolen and worsted mills—as well as dyeing and finishing plants. While at the Esmond Mills, he became the president of the local union. Experiencing firsthand the difficulties endured by many hardworking people, particularly the many that composed the immigrant population, Sgambato decided to try to make a positive difference in their lives. He focused his attention on improving the human condition, and politics became his reform vehicle of choice. So, in 1934, Sgambato sought, and was elected to, a seat on the North Providence Town Council. There he learned the subtleties of politics and the arts of compromise and persuasion. In 1935, Frank joined the labor movement as an organizer. His lifelong career with the United Textile Workers of America would see Sgambato achieve the high honor of election as its international vice-president. He was also made a New England director in 1944.

In 1940, Sgambato was elected to the Rhode Island Senate and took his seat in the January 1941 session. He immediately assumed a prominent role in Senate deliberations. He became a very active proponent of various labor bills and is credited with authoring the Rhode Island Labor Relations Act. He also sponsored two bills to improve retirement benefits for workers and pushed for passage of a state minimum wage law. He chaired the Senate Labor Committee for seven years, between 1949 and 1956. In addition, Sgambato became chairman of the Senate Judiciary Committee and served for four years as deputy majority leader. As a sign of the respect and esteem in which his colleagues held him, Senator Sgambato was chosen to lead his party as Senate majority leader in 1963, a position he held until 1972. In that year, the seventy-one-year-old retired from the Senate after a thirty-two-year career in that chamber.

The year before, Sgambato had retired from his position with the Textile Workers of America. But his departure from active employment with the

Union and from public service in the Senate did not mean that Frank would not continue to be a positive influence in Rhode Island. During various stages of his life, Senator Sgambato served as chairman of the Commission on Interstate Cooperation and was a member of the Industrial Code Commission, the Council of Defense, the Public Transit Authority and the PTA's Legislative Council, on which he served as chairman. He was a member of the Rhode Island Blue Cross Board of Directors and the Providence Lodge No. 14 of the Benevolent and Protective Order of Elks. He was an officer of the Centredale Fire Department and a member of the Knights of Columbus.

On June 18, 1988, the North Providence Town Council, in an impressive ceremony, honored Senator Sgambato by naming the Council Chambers on the second floor of the Frank C. Angell Memorial Town Hall after him. The very room where his public service career began, about eighty years ago, will forever be known as the Frank Sgambato Town Council Chamber.

Frank Sgambato died at the Golden Crest Nursing Center on Friday, January 11, 2002, at the age of 101. He left a daughter, Carmel Gibbons; a brother, John; eight grandchildren; fifteen great-grandchildren; and four great-great-grandchildren. But in a larger sense, Senator Sgambato left us so much more. He left for all Rhode Islanders a legacy of compassion and hard work. He bequeathed a voice to all those in our labor force who had no voice with which to speak for themselves. He left a reason for Italian Americans of all walks, from one end of the state to the other, to believe that anyone who cares about people enough can make a positive difference regardless of personal wealth and physical stature.

Sgambato was waked at the Elliott Robbins Chapel in Centredale and was buried at St. Ann Cemetery in Cranston following services from St. Lawrence Church. In an interview with *Providence Journal* reporter M. Charles Bakst following his retirement from the Senate, Sgambato was asked how he would like to be remembered for his time in public office. He replied, "I was always ready to help people...I'd like to be remembered as one who was helpful and could get along with others." Indeed, he always will be.

JOHN A. NOTTE JR.:
RHODE ISLAND'S COMMON MAN GOVERNOR

There have been only a handful of general officers who have called the town of North Providence home. The first was Lieutenant Governor Elisah Brown, who held the office from 1765 to 1767. The most recent is A. Ralph

Governor Notte (front right) having a good time at the expense of popular entertainer Jimmy Durante (front center), while staff members and other officials join in the jocularity. *Courtesy of the Rhode Island State Archives, 1995-472, Office of the Governor.*

Mollis, who was elected secretary of state in 2006. In between there has been Attorney General Herbert DiSimone, Lieutenant Governor Louis Cappelli and Governor John Notte. To date, however, only one of these men has attained the state's highest office and has had the distinction of having a park named in his honor. Yes, Governor John Notte Park was named after a real person who brought dignity and honor, albeit not without controversy, to the town that he called home for the better part of his life.

John A. Notte Jr. was born in Providence on May 3, 1909, the son of John A. and Eva T. (Rodina) Notte. Young John attended Classical High School and excelled in athletics. During the 1920s, Notte played on a barnstorming team alongside such Yankee greats as Babe Ruth and Lou Gehrig. His talents were noted by athletic administrators, and John was named to the all-state baseball and hockey teams as a second baseman and goalie, respectively. Upon graduation from Classical, Notte attended Providence College on baseball and hockey scholarships and matriculated in 1931. As a young man,

Biographies

John had an insatiable thirst for education, and though he briefly considered a career in professional baseball, he instead quenched his thirst for knowledge by attending Cornell University (1931–32), ultimately graduating with a JD (*juris doctor*, or doctor of laws) from the Boston University School of Law in 1935. In 1934, while still a student in his final year of law school, Notte entered another great institution when he married Marie Joan Huerth, also an attorney. The couple went on to have two children, John III and Joyce. Notte's interest in sports never waned, however, and in the 1940s, he became a part owner of the Providence Greys minor-league baseball team.

In 1936, Notte was admitted to the Rhode Island Bar and, a year later, was named town solicitor in North Providence. The experience of serving the legal needs of a growing community like North Providence most assuredly played a key role in sparking John's interest in government.

Not long after the Japanese attack on Pearl Harbor, John answered the call to serve his country in World War II. He joined the navy, where his leadership ability was recognized; this resulted in his being promoted to the rank of lieutenant. Before being honorably discharged in 1946, Notte participated in the invasions of Anzio, Italy, and southern France.

Upon rejoining civilian life, Notte both resumed his career in law and pursued his interest in government, which led to a 1947 appointment by Governor John O. Pastore to chair the Rhode Island Veterans Bonus Board. Although serving well in that post, he resigned one year later to join the staff of Senator Theodore Francis Green, a position he held until 1957.

In that year, Notte entered the political arena, announcing his intention to run for the office of secretary of state. The Democrat was easily elected to office and served a full two-year term before successfully running for lieutenant governor in 1958. Notte served under Republican governor Christopher DelSesto, who at that time was the only Republican since Rhode Island's "Bloodless Revolution" of 1935 to serve in that office.

The groundwork for a run for the state's highest office had been laid, and now the die would be cast. The fifty-year-old lawyer and military and political leader, after spending some fifteen years of his adult life in the education of the nuances of state politics and government affairs, determined that the time was right to propel himself into a gubernatorial campaign.

Notte's campaign for governor in 1960 was typical of the rough-and-tumble ethnic politics that have come to symbolize Rhode Island elections. The race between the two Italian Americans turned into a statement about ethnicity as much as anything else. Even as a candidate for secretary of state four years earlier, according to historian Matthew J. Smith, Notte had been vocally abusive toward gubernatorial candidate Chris DelSesto, accusing him of being a "figurehead, implying that the Republican Party had never been friendly to the Italian." In the end, however, Notte would prevail by a margin of 227,318 votes to 174,044, and on January 3, 1961, John A. Notte Jr. was sworn into office as Rhode Island's sixty-fifth governor.

His term of office was met with mixed reviews. While Notte was successful in establishing the state's first family court, holding the first one-day, one-place Democratic and Republican primaries that are so much a part of today's electoral process and creating a state division of metropolitan government, he also faced some insurmountable challenges that would dictate his future in political service.

Late in the summer of 1962, he called the General Assembly into special session to reapportion the House of Representatives after the Rhode Island Supreme Court had ruled it necessary. The House was unable to bring about a plan that was acceptable to the court, however, causing Notte to be criticized by some as an ineffective chief executive. Also at issue was the initiation of a state income tax, something that Notte viewed as essential to solving the state's economic problems. The legislature rejected the idea but did, after much debate, pass two other tax bills that Notte had proposed. Notte quickly vetoed them, however, saying that he had changed his mind and was now convinced that they would be bad for the state. In fact, he went on to become the only governor in some twenty years to complete an entire term without a tax increase.

His refusal to raise taxes necessary to fund pet projects and his approval of nighttime horse racing at Lincoln Downs angered the unions. In 1962, Notte became the first Democrat since 1930 to run for governor without the official support of the state's labor unions. Although popular with the people, the lack of union support, his initial support of a state income tax and the youth and charisma of his thirty-nine-year-old Republican opponent, John H. Chafee, took a toll on the Notte campaign effort. The hard-fought battle came down to 7,000 absentee ballots that ultimately decided the contest. In one of the closest elections in Rhode Island gubernatorial history, Notte was defeated 163,952 votes to 163,554, a margin of just 398 votes. When in 1971 the state did finally adopt an income tax, Notte said he felt "'vindicated" and called the income tax "the basis of a good tax structure."

Following his loss in 1962, Notte returned to the private practice of law. He did make one final try for elective office in 1967 when he ran for Congress to fill the vacancy created by the death of John E. Fogarty. Although he lost the primary, his service career was not over. Notte became president of the

Aurora Civic Association and was a member of the Veterans of Foreign Wars, American Legion, Knights of Columbus, the Franciscan Mission Associates, the Italian-American War Veterans and other civic organizations. In 1981, Notte received the Exemplary Citizenship Award from Providence College.

On Monday, March 7, 1983, just days after celebrating his seventy-third birthday, John A. Notte Jr. died of heart failure following a six-month illness. His body lay in state in the rotunda of the statehouse before a celebration of a Christian Mass at SS. Peter and Paul Cathedral and internment at St. Francis Cemetery in Pawtucket.

Controversy continued to follow Governor Notte even into death, however, when on February 20, 2009, the *Providence Journal* printed a news story alleging that Notte was paid a $25,000 bribe by organized crime figures early in his term of office as governor. The allegation stemmed from conversations between mob bosses gleaned from FBI tapes planted in the office of a local mob boss over a three-year period. The allegations were never proven, and there is no evidence that bribe money was ever offered or accepted.

Despite attempts to tarnish his reputation, John Notte Jr. stands today as one of the most honest and compassionate people ever to hold public office. At the time of his passing, then governor J. Joseph Garrahy called him "a man of quiet courage, a man of genuine dignity…an honest man who worked hard to make Rhode Island a better and more compassionate state. That will stand as his highest achievement." Indeed it will.

THE SAGA OF LYDIA WILCOX

Lydia Wilcox is one of those intriguing characters in Centredale history. She didn't change the world in any significant way, but she did have an indelible impact on the lives of those with whom she had come in direct contact. Hers is a story about one of those "neighborhood" characters. You know the type. Just about every community has one. Eighteenth-century Centredale was no exception.

So strongly did Frank C. Angell feel about the tale of Lydia Wilcox that he was compelled to dedicate an entire chapter to her in his book, writing, "The history of Centredale would be incomplete without the story of that remarkable and mysterious person, Miss Lydia Wilcox." It is only fitting, therefore, that her story be recounted here. So sit back, relax and meet Lydia Wilcox.

During the late summer of 1828, James Anthony, the proprietor of the newly constructed Centredale Mill, traveled by horse and carriage to Boston

This is the Wilcox home as it appears today. After her death, ownership reverted to the town. The home was initially expanded and converted to Centredale's first fire station. Subsequently, the building was used as the town's office of zoning and planning. Today, the recycling coordinator occupies the building. *Photo taken by the author.*

on one of his routine business trips. Such trips could take about ten days or so in those days, and Anthony made the trek often, generally alone. During his return trip, he encountered a young, attractive woman walking in his direction. Succumbing to the loneliness, and as was customary at the time, Anthony offered the young woman a ride as far as Centredale, his final destination. In the course of their chatter, the woman revealed to him that she was a millworker. In a moment of impulsivity uncharacteristic of Anthony's normal demeanor, he offered the young woman, a total stranger, a position in the Centredale Cotton Mill.

Once in Centredale, Miss Lyddy, as she became known, took up board with the elderly Rebecca Smith, a resident of the village. Later, however, Lyddy rented three rooms from Smith in the basement of her 1999 Smith Street home. Wilcox worked in the mill for many years and on June 17, 1843, was able to purchase the house from her savings. She resided there for some thirty-four years, until her death.

Although a very attractive woman, Wilcox had a reputation of "strict rectitude." For this reason, she seldom dated, and as a result, the mystery about her became more prominent. As she grew older, Wilcox's personality grew even more peculiar. She began to smoke a clay pipe and oddly dress in calico gowns years after they were no longer the fashion. With her winter hood and summer sunbonnet, her head was always covered, even when she worked indoors. A tightly tied shawl completed Miss Lyddy's odd attire.

At times, Miss Lyddy kept a cow, pigs and hens both for income and enjoyment. She loved animals of all sorts and took exceptional pride in seeing the birth of young pups, calves and just about any livestock, except perhaps those of people she didn't particularly like. On these occasions, she was known to stamp her feet and yell, "Blast him, he never owned a good horse or cow in his life, blast him!" Angell records that her vengeful nature and dark complexion led some to believe that she may have been either a gypsy or a Canadian. More than likely, however, she was of English descent.

On the evening of November 1, 1877, neighbors saw smoke coming from the windows of Miss Lyddy's home. The people of the village rushed into the house and entered her bedroom, where they found her unconscious body lying on the straw bed, which was still engulfed in flames. When the fire was extinguished, Miss Lyddy was removed to the outside, where her low, barely audible moans could be heard for only a short time before she breathed her last. It was supposed that a candle was knocked over when she moved during her sleep.

Her body was brought across Powder-Mill Road (the original name of Smith Street) to Armory Hall, and it was there that her charred remains were prepared for burial. On November 3, 1877, Reverend Donovan presided at her service. Because Wilcox had no heirs, ownership of her home reverted to the town after the legally prescribed thirty years had passed. Thus, Miss Lyddy died much the same as she lived—alone and shrouded in mystery.

On November 1, 1907, the town took possession of the building, which was eventually converted for use as the first volunteer fire station in Centredale. When a new police and fire complex was dedicated by the town in the 1970s, the Wilcox building was used to house other town offices. Although the building still stands, it has undergone several transformations. Recently, its use as the town's planning and zoning headquarters was abandoned when the town purchased and renovated the Golden Dragon Restaurant next to the Police and Fire Complex on Mineral Spring Avenue and relocated those departments to the new site. Most residents of the town know that this building was the first Centredale Fire Station. Now you know it was home to one of Centredale's more colorful characters, Lydia Wilcox.

MARY ANN ANGELL YOUNG: PIONEER AND WOMAN OF FAITH

If not for her marriage to Brigham Young, the details of the life of this indomitable woman might have been lost to history forever. As it happens, however, Mary Ann's remarkable journey stands as a testament to the extraordinary hardships experienced in life by pioneer women in the nineteenth century.

Mary Ann, the third child of North Providence resident James William Angell (born on October 5, 1776, in North Providence) and his wife, Phebe Ann Morton Angell (born 1802 in Florence, Oneida County, New York), entered the world on June 8, 1803, in Seneca, Ontario, New York, while the family was traveling. In 1810, however, James returned to North Providence with his young family where Phebe gave birth to the last six of the couple's ten children.

The Angells were deeply religious, god-fearing people, and once in North Providence, Mary Ann joined the Free Will Baptist Church, developing a keen interest in the Bible. Engrossed by the study of scriptures, especially the prophecies, "She resolved never to marry until she should meet a man of God." One spring day in 1830, while attending a sermon given by Mormon Elder Thomas B. Marsh in nearby Providence, she requested a "copy of the sacred book," testifying many times that the book had changed her life. Two years later, she journeyed to New York to investigate the new religion firsthand. It was then that she was baptized in the faith. In 1833, she ventured west to Kirtland, Ohio, to gather with other saints (as members of the Mormon faith were known) to hear Brigham Young, an apostle of the Mormon Church, preach. "Instinctively she felt drawn towards him, and...admired him so much, that when...he asked her to be his wife she unhesitatingly consented, feeling confident that he was her true mate." They were married on February 18, 1834. Brigham had two children from a previous marriage to Miriam Angeline Works, who had died of consumption seventeen months earlier.

Brigham Young was an energetic and charismatic man who was no stranger to hardship. He had traveled from his native Vermont to Kirtland, Ohio, in 1832 to meet Joseph Smith, the prophet and founder of the Mormon Church of Latter-Day Saints. (Being ordained, he became a leader of the church in 1844 after Smith was murdered. He later led the exodus of the saints to the Salt Lake City Valley, where he became president of the Mormon Church in 1847 and served as governor of the Territory of Utah for eight years beginning in 1850.)

The married couple experienced perilous times that included sickness and attacks from religious bigots. After Brigham cut off from the church forty dissenters, the angry mob retaliated with death threats, causing him to flee Kirtland under cover of darkness on December 22, 1837. Mary Ann was left to fend for herself and their children, which now numbered five. Apostates terrorized them, ransacking their home and threatening her life, all of which caused her health to deteriorate. By February 1838, Mary Ann, who had by now contracted tuberculosis, gathered her children and their few possessions and fled Kirtland to rejoin her husband in Missouri. Along the way, her young daughter Mary fell from the wagon. The massive wagon wheel ran over the child's head, causing seemingly severe injuries. Mary Ann calmly gathered the child in her arms and, praying intensely, carefully shaped the little girl's head back into place, saving the child's life. The family finally rejoined Brigham, who, upon seeing her, exclaimed, "You look as if you were almost in your grave." He nursed her back to health, and life seemingly started to get better. By October, however, tensions and hostilities between the saints and Missourians peaked, causing the Young family and more than eight hundred saints to move on to Illinois. Most had to walk since their wagons and animals had been confiscated. During the three-month ordeal, Mary Ann and her children were forced to live in eleven different quarters.

In late September 1839, church business required Brigham to travel to England. Despite her sixth child being only ten days old, Mary Ann, reminiscent of the Spartan women of old, told Brigham, "Go and fill your mission, and the Lord will bless you, and I will do the best I can for myself and the children." It was while she was without him that a harsh winter forced her and her children to the brink of starvation. For the cause of feeding her family, she decided to cross the Mississippi in search of food. Suffering from malaria and wearing only a thin cotton dress, she rowed across the river with her crying and starving infant by her side, wrapped in a blanket. Once across, a friend fed her and the baby. That friend later wrote, "I'll never forget how she looked, shivering with cold and thinly clad. ...She came back [from the tithing office] with a few potatoes and a little sack [of] flour, for which she seemed very grateful, and...weak as she was from ague [a nineteenth-century disease characterized by alternating chills, fever and sweating] and fever, wended her way to the river bank to row home again."

A year later, Brigham returned home from England suffering from scarlet fever. With winter chill again in the air, Brigham endured high fevers for eighteen days. "I was...so near gone that I could not close my eyes," Brigham wrote, "and my breath stopped. [Mary Ann] threw some cold water in my face; that having no effect, she dashed a handful of strong camphor [a strong odorous substance] into my face and eyes, which I did not feel in the least...She then held my nostrils…and placing her mouth directly over mine, blew into my lungs until she filled them with air. This set my lungs in motion again, and I began to breathe." That inspired treatment, while a common resuscitative technique today, was not known to medicine until the twentieth century.

Mary Ann was very devoted to God and believed that her husband was his messenger. It is that devotion that led her, in 1842, to grant Brigham the permission he sought to enter into the practice of plural marriage. Despite polygamy causing her great pain, she dutifully ministered to many of the fifty-three other "wives" he eventually took, as well as the forty-nine children they bore him as if they were her own. Most of those "wives" and their children affectionately referred to Mary Ann as "Mother Young."

Before long, opposition to the saints in Illinois started to mount, and the family again found it necessary to move farther west, this time settling in Nebraska. It was along this westward journey, and in the encampment that followed, that Mary Ann used her reputation as a "healer" to nurse several sickly saints back to health, earning her the name "Angel of Mercy." When Brigham began his journey to Utah in the spring of 1847, Mary Ann stayed behind to minister to the saints in Nebraska. A year later, Brigham returned to Nebraska to collect his family, and together they all made the trek to the Great Salt Lake Valley, arriving in Utah in September 1848. There, despite the privations and trials of the past, the family prospered, rose to positions of prominence and enjoyed many years of success until Brigham's death on August 29, 1877.

Mary Ann survived her husband by five years, but just three years after his death, Mary Ann's ailments returned, causing her great suffering. In March 1881, her feet began to swell, making walking too painful an exercise. Within weeks, the excruciating conditions of the affliction began to spread to the rest of her body. She "lingered in great agony" until nine o'clock on the evening of June 27, 1882, when, at the age of seventy-nine, she expired, leaving behind her three surviving children. Despite the tribulations in her life, Mary Ann demonstrated an unshakable reliance on the Lord. A *New York Times* article eulogized her, noting, "Ever cheerful and buoyant she passed through a host of hardships with extraordinary steadiness and acceptance, always [looking] upward from whence help would come."

After her death, saints from all over the United States made annual pilgrimages to North Providence just to view the home where Mary Ann's values were shaped. Those pilgrimages continued until that home no longer stood. Such was the esteem that marked Mary Ann's value to the Mormon community.

Part III

Walking Tours of the Villages of Lymansville, Allendale, Centredale and Fruit Hill

The First North Providence Heritage Walking Tour

Heritage Stop 1
Lymansville Mill Complex
184 Woonasquatucket Avenue

Daniel Lyman was born in Durham, Connecticut, in 1756, the son of Thomas Lyman. He was commissioned as a captain in the Continental army while still a student at Yale College. He served in many battles, including the Battle of Ticonderoga, and was the first to greet Comte de Rochambeau and his French troops upon their arrival in Newport on July 11, 1780. He was married just two years later to Mary "Polly" Wanton of Newport, Rhode Island. Lyman acted as a surveyor for the port of Newport and engaged in the practice of law. From 1802 to 1816, Lyman served as chief justice of the Rhode Island Supreme Court.

In 1807, in anticipation of his retirement, Lyman began to purchase large tracts of land in North Providence, some eighty acres in all. One parcel's chain of title includes William McGee and Richard Whipple, the great-grandson of Benjamin Whipple. Lyman retired to a country seat in North Providence in 1808. In 1809, William Goddard of Providence granted him the rights to build a dam along the Woonasquatucket River. On July 1, 1809, Lyman organized the Lyman Cotton Manufacturing Company and started construction on a mill that became operational about twenty months later. Aside from the distinction of being the oldest mill built within the current

The Lyman Mill as it appeared in 2009. The mill complex is currently being considered for conversion to apartments and condominiums. *Photo by author.*

boundaries of North Providence, the Lyman Mill was the first in Rhode Island to use water-powered Scotch looms in the weaving of cotton.

Daniel and Polly Lyman had thirteen children. Son Henry B. Lyman inherited the Lyman Mill upon Daniel's death on October 16, 1830. His daughter, Harriet Hazzard, whose husband, Benjamin, served in the Rhode Island General Assembly for thirty-two years, inherited the family home in Newport, which has been known since as the Wanton-Lyman-Hazard House.

Continue along the left side of Woonasquatucket Avenue toward Centredale, eight-tenths of a mile to the Allendale Mill.

Heritage Stop 2
Allendale Mill Complex
492 Woonasquatucket Avenue

Zachariah Allen was born in Providence on September 15, 1795. He graduated from Brown University and began the practice of law in 1815. By 1817, he was married to the former Eliza Harriet Arnold. Dissatisfied with his law practice, he became interested in the textile industry. An inventor, Allen also had a keen

Walking Tours of the Villages of Lymansville, Allendale, Centredale and Fruit Hill

The Allendale Mill was the first in America to be constructed with fire-retardant materials. Zachariah Allen thought that this would lead to lower fire insurance rates. Instead, it led to the founding of the insurance giant FM Global. *Photo reprinted from* The Annals of Centredale *by Frank C. Angell.*

interest in the technology of the textile industry, including refined power looms and cloth finishing machinery. Allen is credited with inventing high-speed shafting with loose belts. In 1821, he developed the first domestic hot-air furnace. In 1833, he patented a cutoff valve for steam engines.

Allen engaged John Holden Greene to build his mill on the Woonasquatucket River in 1822. The wool mill employed several unique fire safety devices, including heavy fire doors, a sprinkler system, a rotary fire pump and a copper-riveted fire hose. Allen also built a heavy firewall separating the picker room from the rest of the mill and set the roof shingles in mortar. Despite his mill at Allendale being the first to employ such fireproof construction, something that reduced the likelihood of damage from a factory fire, which was so prevalent in the period, insurance companies refused to provide a discount in his policy premium. Angered, Allen founded the Manufacturer's Mutual, a factory insurance company that helped other factory owners develop methods to prevent fires and other factory disasters. His insurance company eventually became known as the Factory

Manufacturers' Company and then Allendale Insurance. The company still exists today under the name FM Global and is headquartered in Johnston. In 1976, the Allendale Mill building was converted to condominiums.

Continue along the left side of Woonasquatucket Avenue toward Centredale, about fifty feet to the Allendale Mill Store.

Heritage Stop 3
Allendale Mill Store/Scout's Hall
498 Woonasquatucket Avenue

In addition to the construction of his mill, Zachariah Allen also built a store on his property in 1822. The country store was used by many of the millworkers to furnish the goods and supplies they needed for daily sustenance. The building was designed in the Greek Revival style, and the store occupied the first floor, while the second floor housed an apartment. In a story typically

described as happening "only in Rhode Island," James Halsey Angell and wife Sarah, another of the town's most prominent residents, occupied the second floor. James worked as an accountant in the mill and as a clerk of the mill store. James's son, Frank C. Angell, one of Centredale's most influential nineteenth- and twentieth-century citizens, was born here in 1845. Frank C. Angell would go on to influence the character of most of Centredale in the latter part of the century and would become a prime mover in the establishment of the town's first library, first Episcopal church and first fraternal organization. In later years, the mill store building was used as Scout's Hall and as a meeting place.

As was the case with most mills constructed in the 1800s, the Allendale Mill included the construction of a mill store. In addition to being a convenience to the millworkers, it was a boon to the mill owner, who profited handsomely from his employees' patronage. When this 1928 photo was taken, the store had been converted to a meeting hall called Scout's Hall. *Photo reprinted from* The Annals of Centredale *by Frank C. Angell.*

Walking Tours of the Villages of Lymansville, Allendale, Centredale and Fruit Hill

Continue along the left side of Woonasquatucket Avenue toward Centredale for about one-tenth of a mile to the first of the Allendale Mill houses.

Heritage Stop 4
Allendale Mill Village Houses
518 Woonasquatucket Avenue

Zachariah Allen has been described as a visionary. This may be why he chose to locate his mills—both the Allendale Mill in North Providence and his Georgiaville Mill (later known as the Bernon Manufacturing Company)—along established turnpikes. But transportation in the mid-1800s was difficult at best, and while the turnpikes may have made it easier to get raw materials to his mill and his goods to market, it didn't do much to help his millworkers get to work each day. To ensure a productive workday, Allen, like other mill owners of the day, established an entire village. Allen's village included the construction of several mill houses for mill employees to occupy. The home pictured here is reflective of the style chosen for a mill house and was built in 1824. The gambrel-style cottage is fairly typical construction for the era but is reflective of the single family

There are several original mill houses still standing within the Allendale Village. This example is located at 518 Woonasquatucket Avenue and was built circa 1824. *Photo by author.*

rather than the duplex-style homes built as part of a common mill village (including Greystone Mill).

Cross to the right side of Woonasquatucket Avenue and walk a few steps toward Centredale to the Allendale Baptist Church.

Heritage Stop 5
The Allendale Baptist Church
545 Woonasquatucket Avenue

With the construction of the mill, the mill store and the mill houses, Zachariah Allen's village was a reality. Allen's genius was responsible for designing an elaborate water supply system that caught and saved floodwaters and powered a mill. He employed more than one hundred people and successfully populated an entire area of the town. But the new townspeople had needs other than work. The year was now 1847, some twenty-five years after the development of the mill. The residents were established and longing for a local place to worship, a place for their children to learn and for other community structure. Again Allen stepped up to the plate. He constructed

Allen's plans to include a library in the Allendale Baptist Church never materialized. Instead, the Sunday school featured a lecture hall. The wooden portion on the right of the structure was a later addition. *Photo by author.*

a stone building not far from the mill to be used as a Sunday school for the children of the millworkers and as a library. The library was never established, however, and the second floor was instead used as a lecture hall. In 1850, the building was consecrated as a church. Zachariah Allen died in 1882 at the age of eighty-seven.

Continue along the right side of Woonasquatucket Avenue toward Centredale for one-tenth of a mile to the home of Frank Sgambato.

Heritage Stop 6
Home of Senator Frank Sgambato
581 Woonasquatucket Avenue

In many ways, Frank Sgambato was just an ordinary man. Yet he was also the embodiment of all Italian Americans in North Providence. Born in New York City in 1901, Sgambato moved with his family to North Providence in 1914 at the age of thirteen. He enlisted in the U.S. Navy and served from 1920 to 1922. He built his home in 1926 and began a political career in 1934, running as a Democrat and winning a seat on the North Providence Town Council, representing District 1. He served as a councilman for five

Frank Sgambato built this house in 1926 when he was twenty-five years old. This photo was taken in 1950. *Courtesy of Jeffrey Gibbons.*

years, choosing to seek election to the Rhode Island Senate in 1939. There he served for thirty-three years and attained the position of majority leader. He retired from the Senate in 1972 and, because of his distinguished service, became the first to be granted the status of majority leader emeritus. During his Senate career, he was very active on labor issues, having worked nearly thirty years as an international vice-president of the United Textile Workers of America. On June 19, 1988, the North Providence Town Council Chamber was dedicated in his honor. Senator Sgambato died on Friday, January 11, 2002, at the age of 101. He was waked at the Elliott Robbins Funeral Home in Centredale and buried from the St. Lawrence Church, the next stop on our tour.

Continue along the right side of Woonasquatucket Avenue toward Centredale for one-tenth of a mile to St. Lawrence Church (Grace Unity Baptist Church).

Heritage Stop 7
Grace Unity Baptist Church (Former St. Lawrence Catholic Church)
Woonasquatucket Avenue

Before the population of North Providence began to grow, Catholics attended mass at St. Thomas Church, some two miles away. This trip, however, became too cumbersome, especially for the infirm and disabled. As their numbers swelled to four hundred, the Catholics of Centredale petitioned Bishop Harkins for a new church. The bishop agreed and appointed the young and energetic Reverend James Hardy the first pastor. Mass was celebrated in a room secured in Allendale until other arrangements could be made. Finally, a suitable site for a new building

Subsequent to a merger with Mary Mother of Mankind Church, St. Lawrence Church celebrated its last Mass on Sunday, October 31, 2011, after 104 years of service to its parishioners. The parish fell victim to hard times, and the remaining parishioners were spread among three other parishes. The building continues as a house of worship and is called the Grace Unity Baptist Church. *Photo by author.*

was purchased, and ground was broken on June 17, 1907. The selected contractor was J.C. Walch & Company, and Fountaine & Kennicut was the chosen architectural firm. It designed a building that was 45 by 100 feet, with a spire reaching 107 feet above ground level.

On October 20, 1907, the cornerstone was laid in an impressive ceremony led by Right Reverend Matthew Harkins and assisted by a large delegation of clergy. Reverend James Hardy held the first service in the unfinished structure on October 8, 1907. In 2011, St. Lawrence celebrated its final mass, having fallen victim to a sagging economy and declining parishioner rolls. The building was sold and is now the home of Grace Unity Baptist Church. The remaining parishioners from St. Lawrence were reassigned to Mary Mother of Mankind in the Woodhaven section of North Providence and St. Augustine's Parish in Providence.

Continue toward Centredale one-tenth of a mile to St. Alban's Episcopal Church.

Heritage Stop 8
St. Alban's Episcopal Church
Smith Street (Route 44)

In 1844, St. Alban's was established as an Episcopal mission in Centredale and held occasional services in the Baptist meetinghouse, which was loaned to Reverend James C. Richmond for use for that purpose. In 1847, Reverend James Eames held regular Sunday open-air services in the village and soon purchased a stone church at Center Mill. Because there were Baptist churches already established in Allendale, Fruit Hill and Graniteville, the Centredale mission was abandoned in 1855. However, services continued to be held occasionally in the meetinghouse even after it was purchased by James H. Angell in 1863 and converted to Armory Hall in order to train Civil War soldiers.

The mission work was revived in 1897 when Frank C. Angell donated land at the "very best location" and, along with William Dracup and Reverend Colwell, served on a building committee for a new church. The first mission service was held in the new church on February 21, 1900. It was dedicated on January 1, 1906, and consecrated on June 16 of that year. It was incorporated as a parish on March 20, 1911. A church hall was built in 1953 to accommodate parish functions. In the 1970s, St. Albans combined with St. James Episcopal Church in Fruit Hill. The merger lasted only a short while, however, because parishioners were alternating services between the two buildings. In May 2012, the Episcopal Church announced plans to combine St. Albans Church with

Although established in 1900, St. Alban's Episcopal Church did not incorporate until some eleven years later. This church, too, is expected to close in 2012. *Postcard, circa 1920, from the author's collection.*

Trinity Episcopal Church of Scituate. The last service held by St. Alban's at this site is scheduled to take place on July 21, 2012. Thereafter, the combined parishioners will hold their services in Scituate.

From Woonasquatucket Avenue, look directly in front of the church to see the World War I memorial.

Heritage Stop 9
World War I Memorial
Woonasquatucket Avenue/Smith Street

The townspeople in North Providence were extremely patriotic. In 1920, there was a strong desire within the community to build a memorial to the veterans of World War I. A piece of land in front of the St. Alban's Church, located directly across the street from Victory Hall (no longer standing), was offered as a site. Victory Hall was built in about 1919 at 1975 Smith Street. The statue is called *On to Victory*, was designed by Warwick sculptor John G. Hardy and was mounted on a large stone donated by Nellie (Appleby) Angell.

Walking Tours of the Villages of Lymansville, Allendale, Centredale and Fruit Hill

This World War I monument, *On to Victory* (seen at right), was dedicated in 1920 and has been a prominent landmark in Centredale since that time. The cannon shown in the foreground was removed when the Centredale bypass was developed by the Department of Transportation. Its whereabouts are unknown. *Postcard photo from author's collection.*

This photo of the World War I monument shows its proximity to St. Alban's Church. It also depicts the "cannon" that was an original part of the monument. *Postcard from the author's collection.*

The monument was dedicated on May 30, 1920, at a ceremony entitled "A Welcome Home Celebration to Our North Providence Veterans."

With your back to the monument, continue on Route 44 into the business district of Centredale one-tenth of a mile to the North Providence Town Hall.

Heritage Stop 10
North Providence Town Hall
2000 Smith Street

Frank C. Angell was an eighth-generation direct descendant of Thomas Angell who left England for Massachusetts in 1631 and in 1636 accompanied Roger Williams to Rhode Island. The son of James Halsey Angell and Sarah Angell Capron, Frank was born on March 9, 1845, in an apartment on the second floor of the Allendale Mill Store. He moved to Centredale as a young boy and remained there his entire life. He attended local public schools, learned the harness maker's trade and, in May 1877, established a store and shop in Centredale. By 1881, he needed more space and built the Masonic Hall, using the entire first floor for his shop. Frank Angell also served as a councilman and tax assessor and was town treasurer

Frank Angell bequeathed his homestead and $10,000 to the town for the construction of a larger town hall. The home was relocated and is still being used as a residence today. *Photo by author.*

for eighteen years. He died on December 12, 1928, and bequeathed his homestead to the town for construction of a new town hall.

At a financial town meeting in 1929, the voters accepted the gift of the homestead and authorized the town council to sell a bond issue of $50,000 to proceed with the erection of a town hall. Ground was broken on November 3, 1930. The building was completed on June 15, 1931. In 1979, the addition seen here was added to accommodate the office of the new mayor. (The first mayor of North Providence, Salvatore Mancini, was elected in 1973 after revisions to the town's legislative charter were approved by the voters and passed by the General Assembly.)

Continue along the left side of Smith Street (Route 44) to the next building, the Capitol Billiards Building.

Heritage Stop 11
The Capital Billiards Building
Centredale Hotel and Tavern
2026 Smith Street

On this site in 1824, James Angell built the Centredale Hotel and Tavern. For some sixty years or so, this building served as the community center. According

The Centredale Hotel was operated by James Angell Jr., then his son, Nathaniel, and ultimately by James Halsey Angell. It was a frequent layover for people traveling from northern Rhode Island to downtown Providence. *Postcard from the collection of Dan Brown.*

to Thomas and Barbara Greene's photographic history of North Providence, the hotel/tavern served as a farmers' clubroom, as well as the post office during the time that James Halsey Angell served as the postmaster (1854–58). Because one could not earn a living solely by operating a post office, it was a usual practice to open a post office as an extension of another business venture. From 1910 to 1915, Emma Baron served as the postmistress from a building located across the street from the hotel (lower right of image). Emma's brother, Charles Baron, succeeded her. When James Angell died in 1870, ownership of his real estate passed to his son, James Halsey Angell. Ownership stayed in the family until August 25, 1897, when it was sold to Cassius Mathewson. Subsequent stores operating from this site include Kane's Drugs, Star Meat Market and Adam's Drug. Capital Billiards celebrated its 100th anniversary in business in 2009. That business was originally located in Providence.

Continue along the left side of Smith Street (Route 44) to the next building, located at 2036–2038 Smith Street (Route 44).

Heritage Stop 12
2036–2038 Smith Street
The Angell Building
Original Site of the A&P Market

This building, one of many in Centredale owned by Frank Angell, was once rented to the A&P supermarket chain. *Photo by author.*

Walking Tours of the Villages of Lymansville, Allendale, Centredale and Fruit Hill

In February 1915, the owner of this building, Frank C. Angell, rented it to the Atlantic and Pacific Grocery Store Chain, also known as A&P. The market occupied the entire building, which is much larger than it looks from the front. The market was managed by Alfred Malone. According to Thomas and Barbara Greene's *History of North Providence*, volume 1, the initial rental payment charged by Angell was five dollars per month. The rent was eventually increased to ten dollars and then to sixteen dollars per month.

Continue along the left side of Smith Street (Route 44) to the next building, occupied by Our Place Tuxedos.

Heritage Stop 13
The Our Place Building
Site of the Free Will Baptist Church, Armory Hall and Broley Hall
2040 Smith Street

On this site in 1832 was built the Free Will Baptist Church. In 1847, the Episcopal Society, which until 1855 held its services here, purchased the property. James Halsey Angell purchased the property in 1863 and used it as Armory Hall, a Civil War military and training complex. After the war,

Our Place Tuxedos & Uniforms occupies the building originally used as a hotel and theater operated by Clarence Broley. Before that, the site housed the Free Will Baptist Church, later converted to Armory Hall before being destroyed by fire. *Photo by author.*

The Free Will Baptist Church as it appeared on this site in 1832. By the Civil War, it was used as an armory to train local Union soldiers. *Photo reprinted from* The Annals of Centredale *by Frank C. Angell.*

it became a public hall, the site of many theatrical productions held from the late 1860s until 1892, when the building and the one next to it were destroyed by fire. Some years later, Clarence Broley purchased the site and constructed the Broley Hall building. The second floor housed Casino Motion Pictures, the town's first movie theater, which was operated by Napoleon Trahan. The first floor was a strip store that housed such establishments as Piggly Wiggly, Reilly Smoke Shop and Mayflower Groceries.

In the 1930s, Napoleon Trahan built the Community Theater, the town's second theater, just down the road on Waterman Avenue. This is the site of the present-day Joe Rendine's Maytag Appliances. It was eventually called the Hillside Theater and later was transformed into an indoor miniature golf course. In the 1970s, it was destroyed by fire as well.

Continue along the left side of Smith Street to the next building, which once housed Tim Hortons.

Heritage Stop 14
Tim Hortons
Site of Edwin Capron's Livery Stable
2046 Smith Street

To the right of Our Place, on a lot partially overlapping the lot on which the former Tim Hortons building lies, is the 1831 site of Edwin Capron's livery stable, the first in Centredale. Capron operated the stable until his death in 1889, when Herbert Sweet took over the operation. Time and technology negated the need for a livery stable, and the Sweets eventually operated

Sweet's Hardware and Gas Station from the site. A successful operation from the 1940s to the early 1950s, the hardware store was closed and sold at a public auction sale on March 2, 1953. The property later served as the site of the Christmas Tree Shop and then the Salvation Army Thrift Shop in the 1960s, as well as Adrian's Restaurant, an upscale dining facility, in the 1970s.

Edwin Capron built Centredale's first livery stable in 1831. *Photo reprinted from* The Annals of Centredale *by Frank C. Angell.*

Between Our Place and the former Tim Hortons building (the original Capron Stable was slightly right of the former Tim Hortons building) were the Broley Hotel and the Broley Café & Bar.

Diagonally across Smith Street and a few feet toward the Johnston line is the Masonic Building.

Heritage Stop 15
The Masonic Temple Building
2121 Smith Street (Route 44)

When the formation of the Roger Williams Lodge No. 32 of the Ancient, Free and Accepted Masons (AF&AM) was being considered on September 15, 1875, about thirty people residing in or around Centredale assembled at the Union Library to plan its organization. James Halsey Angell, a member of Temple Lodge No. 18, presided. His son, Frank, was elected secretary. The lodge name was formally adopted at a meeting held on December 27, 1875. The grand master of the Rhode Island Grand Lodge, Nicholas Van Slyck, granted permission for the new lodge on January 27, 1876. The first meeting of the Centredale Lodge was held in the Railroad Hall building on March 4, 1876. Rhode Island Supreme Court judge George M. Carpenter delivered an appropriate address at the impressive ceremonies of the constitution on May 27, 1876, followed by the election of officers. Frank C. Angell served as the lodge secretary for more than thirty years. In 1885, with membership

The cornerstone for the Masonic Temple was laid in 1929 by the Ancient, Free and Accepted Masons, with funds bequeathed by Frank C. Angell, a longtime member of the Roger Williams Lodge No. 32. Today, the building is used by the Neuva Generacion Christiana (NGC) Church. *Photo by author.*

reaching 112, the lodge meetings were moved to larger quarters in Angell block at 2005 Smith Street. This building was erected in 1929, the year following the death of Frank C. Angell, with funds received in part from Angell's bequest. The longest-serving member of the lodge never got to see the purchase of the land or the construction of the building that the lodge called home for many years.

Walk back to the corner, follow the curve of the road to Waterman Avenue, turn left and walk in a westerly direction to 46–48 Waterman Avenue.

Heritage Stop 16
Centredale Mill House
46–48 Waterman Avenue

Like the villages of Lymansville, Allendale and Greystone, Centredale was also a mill village. The "Centre Mill" was started by Israel Arnold on land he purchased in 1812. This site is currently occupied by the senior citizen Brook Village high rise. In 1823, Richard Anthony purchased a half interest in the Centre Mill in Centredale from Israel Arnold. Just three years later, his son,

As with most nineteenth-century mill construction, a village was established to house the millworkers and to serve their needs. The photo shows the last mill house remaining from the Centredale Mill Village. *Photo by author.*

James, purchased the other half interest, and together Richard and James operated the mill under the name Richard Anthony & Son. Together, the Anthonys constructed a mill village consisting of several mill houses and the first store in Centredale operated by Richard's son-in-law, Luther Carpenter, who married James's sister, Mary Elizabeth.

The original mill building was destroyed by fire in 1850. James Cuniff built a new mill in 1853 but sold it to Amos Beckwith, owner of the Dyerville Mill, in 1859. In 1889, this mill was partially destroyed when a fire broke out on the third story the building.

By this time, the mill industry was down, and the building was sold in 1891 to Henry H. Green and his partners. By 1910, the mill was owned by William Dracup, William Mackey and James Lister Jr. These owners also abandoned the manufacture of cotton and began producing worsted yarn. As was usually the case when mills were developed, a mill village was established. The home pictured here is the last remaining mill house from that village. Dracup, who resided at 1336 Smith Street, died on February 5, 1919.

Walk one-tenth of a mile in an easterly direction on Waterman Avenue to the junction of Smith Street.

Heritage Stop 17
Sak's Centredale Liquors
Site of the Centredale Cotton Mill Store
Junction of Smith and Waterman

James and Richard Anthony, the owners of the Greystone Mill, purchased an interest in the Centredale Cotton Mill in 1826 from Israel Arnold. In addition to their many mill improvements, they established a mill store on this site. The small one-story building, the first store in Centredale, was torn down in 1892. As travel to Providence was difficult in those days, this factory store was a place where mill employees could purchase the everyday items they might have needed. Shortly after its opening, Anthony hired Luther Carpenter as his clerk/salesman. Carpenter was described by Frank C. Angell as "one of the most successful men, from a business standpoint, that Centredale has had."

Carpenter eventually married James Anthony's daughter, Mary. A few months later, Anthony gave the store to Carpenter, who turned it into a most successful enterprise. As more space was now needed, Carpenter purchased

Saks of Centredale, a long-established family business in its own right, occupies the site of the Centredale Mill store owned by the Anthonys and successfully operated by Luther Carpenter after his marriage to Mary Anthony. *Photo by author.*

a lot at the corner of Smith Street and Mineral Spring Avenue. Five years later, in 1847, Carpenter erected a building on that lot and moved the store into it. He continued to run the country/variety store at the new location until his death on October 7, 1886. The store was then sold to nineteen-year-old George T. Batchelder, one of Carpenter's employees.

Walk a few yards in an easterly direction on Smith Street and turn left onto Mineral Spring Avenue.

Heritage Stop 18
Elliott Robbins Funeral Home
2251 Mineral Spring Avenue

When Frank C. Angell died in 1928, he bequeathed his homestead to the town for the construction of a town hall. One of the outbuildings on his property was a large two-story barn. In 1930, Harry Sharp, an entrepreneur from Centredale and a town councilman in the mid-1920s, purchased the barn and moved it a few hundred yards to the northwest on what is now the beginning of Mineral Spring Avenue. Sharp renovated the barn and

Councilman Harry Sharp purchased Frank Angell's barn, moved it to this site and converted it to a family home. When his daughter, Elsie, married an undertaker, Sharp gave them the home to use as a funeral parlor. Elsie, an icon in her own right, passed away at the age of ninety-two on December 10, 2011. *Photo by author.*

converted it to be used as his family home. Eventually, Harry's daughter, Elsie, married Elliott Robbins, an undertaker. In 1948, Harry gave his new son-in-law the house for use as a funeral parlor. Though the building has been extended many times, the original roofline of the Angell barn is distinguishable on the front part of the building. Elliott and Elise's daughter, Lynne, also married an undertaker. Geoffrey Green, Lynne's husband, now runs the funeral home. Elsie M. Sharp Robbins passed away at the age of ninety-two on December 12, 2011.

Look to the left of the funeral home. This was the site of the first public library in North Providence.

Heritage Stop 19
Lot to the Left of Elliott Robbins Funeral Home
Mineral Spring Avenue

By the summer of 1868, the two hundred inhabitants of Centredale had grown tired of the long stagecoach trip to the Providence library. Frank C. Angell, Marcus M. Joslin and Alexander W. Harrington felt that it was time to establish a free public library in town. To raise the necessary $200 to supply the library with books, a series of local entertainments was held. The first performance, *All Is Not Gold That Glitters*, was held in Armory Hall on Saturday evening, October 31, 1868. After just four months, they raised the first installment of $100. Subscriptions brought the total to $400.

On April 21, 1869, a permanent committee was formed, with Frank Angell serving as secretary and John Marsh as chairman. On May 13, the

This photo shows how the town's first public library, established by Frank C. Angell and others, looked shortly after completion. *Photo reprinted from* The Annals of Centredale *by Frank C. Angell.*

constitution and bylaws were passed, and the society was called the Union
Library Association. Frank Angell was named librarian. That year's Fourth
of July celebration was used as a fundraiser, with enough money raised to
secure a ninety-nine-year lease on a new twenty- by twenty-six-foot, single-
story building. Ground was broken in March 1870, and after completion,
$400 remained for the purchase of books. The ladies, meeting at the home
of Nathaniel Angell, also organized bake sales and a successful fair, netting
a "handsome sum." The library was dedicated on July 4, 1870, with 350
volumes adorning the shelves. The number of volumes had increased to
5,000 by 1909, 6,000 by 1925 and more than 14,000 by 2008.

Continue on the left side of Mineral Spring Avenue to the next structure,
Yacht Club Beverage.

Heritage Stop 20
Yacht Club Beverage
2239 Mineral Spring Avenue

Prominent Centredale businessman Harry Sharp emigrated from England in
1906. On December 12, 1907, he opened his first business, a fish and chips

Harry Sharp traveled to England to learn how to produce carbonated drinks. The pre-1920
business he founded upon his return to North Providence has been operated on this site ever
since. *Photo by author.*

restaurant, across from town hall. In 1912, he purchased land on Mineral Spring Avenue and built four stores. In 1915, he returned to England to learn the carbonated beverage business. Upon his return, he started a business he called Harry Sharp, Manufacturer of Mineral Water & Aerated Drinks at 2253 Mineral Spring Avenue. He later renamed it the Yacht Club Bottling Works. While the official name is Bottling Company, the business was later sold and was eventually purchased by John Sgambato in 1961. John had worked at the facility for twenty-five years before deciding to purchase it. John's son, Bill, also started working there in the 1960s and eventually took control of the operation from his dad. Today, Yacht Club Bottling Works is still owned and operated by Bill Sgambato and his sons, Michael and John. The founder, Harry Sharp, was also very prominent in town affairs and served for several years on the North Providence Town Council.

Walk straight ahead across the bypass and immediately turn to the right and cross Mineral Spring Avenue to the Old Town Hall and Jail.

Heritage Stop 21
Old Town Hall and Jail
2226 Mineral Spring Avenue

In February 1765, farmers who were upset that the Providence Council passed laws benefiting only the industrialized sections of town petitioned the General Assembly for status as a new and separate town. The request was answered, and on June 13, 1765, the town of North Providence was established, with the village of Pawtucket being the seat of the new government. On March 27, 1874, a portion of North Providence was annexed to Pawtucket and another portion was returned to Providence, creating the town boundaries as they exist today. At this point, town meetings were generally

This was the seat of government in North Providence from 1879 until 1931, when operations were moved into the new building at 2000 Smith Street. The old jail cells are still in the basement of this building. *Photo reprinted from The Annals of Centredale by Frank C. Angell.*

held in Armory Hall. On June 2, 1879, it was decided to build a town hall designating Centredale the seat of government. Various sections of the town, in a spirited debate, fought vigorously for that honor. The lot on Mineral Spring Avenue was secured, and with $2,000, a two-story, twenty-eight- by thirty-six-foot building was erected. The police station was located in the basement, with four detention cells for prisoners. The town clerk's office, town sergeant's office and the council chambers were located on the first floor, while the second floor was used for meetings. The building is still owned by the town today and is used to house the town historian. Tours are available by appointment.

Directly behind the Old Town Hall is the old E.A. Brayton School.

Heritage Stop 22
E.A. Brayton School Building
2 Thomas Street (Corner of Angell)

The first school in Centredale was built at the corner of Steere Avenue and Smith Street, diagonally across from the current town hall, sometime between 1802 and 1805. By 1848, the village, with a burgeoning mill population,

Centredale's third school building is vacant in 2012 after code enforcement issues forced its last tenant to vacate in 2009. *Photo by author.*

had outgrown that building, and the second school was built on Angell Avenue. The original building was moved to Woonasquatucket Avenue and converted for residential use. Continued population growth necessitated the construction of an addition to the second school building in 1886. By the 1920s, the Centredale School had once again become overcrowded, and in 1930, a new school was built on Angell Avenue. The E.A. Brayton School became the fourth school built in Centredale. It was named after E. Antoinette Brayton, who retired in 1925 after fifty years of service as a teacher, forty-one of those years having been served at Centredale schools.

Cross back to the left side of Mineral Spring Avenue and continue east one-tenth of a mile to Sweet Street, turn left and walk to the end. The last house on the right at the corner of Sweet Street and Walter Avenue is 20 Walter Avenue.

Heritage Stop 23
Frank C. Angell House
20 Walter Avenue

Frank C. Angell bequeathed his homestead to the Town of North Providence for the construction of the new town hall. In preparation of the site, his

Frank C. Angell's 1880 home was relocated to this site following his death so as to make room for the construction of a more appropriately sized town hall. *Photo by author.*

home was sold and moved through a field and onto its present location at 20 Walter Avenue. The handsome Victorian structure, with mansard roof construction, was built in 1880 and relocated in 1929. Frank C. Angell died in 1928 and is buried in the North Burial Ground that was at one time within the boundaries of North Providence. Historical Cemetery No. 3, located directly across Sweet Street from the site of his home, is the resting place of Frank's father, James Halsey Angell, and his mother, Sarah Angell Capron, as well as many other members of the Angell family. There is no doubt that without Frank C. Angell, the face of Centredale would be much different today.

Directly across the street from the Frank C. Angell House is North Providence Historical Cemetery No. 3.

Heritage Stop 24
Historical Cemetery No. 3

A small lot of land, located at the corner of Walter Avenue and Sweet Street, is the final resting place of many of Frank C. Angell's relatives, including his paternal grandparents, James Angell and Selinda Ray Angell, James's second wife. Frank C. Angell's mother, Sarah Angell Capron, and her parents, Edwin and Deborah (Angell) Capron, are also resting here. This historical cemetery also is the final resting place of many other prominent citizens of eighteenth- and nineteenth-century Centredale. Many of the gravestones have been destroyed by vandals over the years. Some have been lost and others buried or partially buried. But enough remains to know that this was the burial site of many of the people who have shaped the social, cultural and political history of Centredale.

Historical Cemetery No. 3 is the final resting place for many prominent Centredale residents, including many members of the Angell family. Nathaniel Angell helped raise funds to start the first library and hosted the organizational meetings at his home. *Photo by author.*

Stop 24 concludes the first North Providence Heritage Tour. The second North Providence Heritage Tour begins about one mile to the east at the north corner of Mineral Spring Avenue and Smithfield Road.

OTHER STOPS OF INTEREST IN THE VILLAGE OF CENTREDALE WITHIN WALKING DISTANCE OF THIS TOUR

After Stop 15, continue along Smith Street in a westerly direction across the bridge into Johnston. The Burger King property on the right is the approximate site of the first railroad station in Centredale, established in 1873. The first passenger train came through on the morning of August 11. The roadbed stretched twenty-three miles. This was also the site of the Revolutionary powder mill operated by Jacob Goff, whose house was located across the street where the school buses are parked.

Back into Centredale, behind and to the right of the Masonic Building, is the site of the old sawmill, the first business established in town. It was built by Captain Richard Arnold circa 1700 "near the southerly end of the dam of the Centredale Worsted Company, about 125' from the highway." The land belonged to Richard Pray. The mill changed ownership many times until Isaac Olney built a gristmill on the west side of the river in 1787 and combined operations. In 1797, Olney sold the mill to William Goddard, who removed the sawmill but continued to operate the gristmill. The gristmill discontinued operation in about 1852. While no Revolutionary War battles were fought in North Providence, the legislature did choose the site to be the state's only powder mill. The state selected Jacob Goff to operate the mill and built a home for him and his family in 1777. On August 28, 1779, a fire and explosion that could be felt many miles away destroyed the mill and cost Goff and his assistant, Laban Beverly, their lives. Isaac Olney later purchased the land.

After Stop 7, taking a right at the fork after St. Lawrence Church will lead to 4 George Street, the Centredale Independent Methodist Church, started by Reverend William H. Tilley. After holding successful open-air services here, the group purchased the lot and built this church, which was dedicated on June 17, 1897. Tilley became the pastor after his June 27, 1901 ordination. Across the street from the church is 9 George Street, the building that housed the town's third library.

Other Stops of Interest in the Village of Greystone Within Walking Distance of This Tour

Stop 16 enters Waterman Avenue, heading in a westerly direction. If you continue in that direction for a distance of two-tenths of a mile, you will be in the village of Greystone. Captain Olney Angell and others developed a mill near the Greystone Social Club in 1813. The club served as a hub of local entertainment and featured swimming, boating and fishing in the Woonasquatucket River Pond. Later, flying lessons were offered in water planes. The mill was purchased in 1816 by Richard Anthony, who built his house at 201 Waterman Avenue in 1818. The stately home still stands today, as does Richard's father James Anthony's home that was constructed just down the road at 156 Waterman Avenue in 1822.

Joseph Westcott purchased the mill in 1835 and enlarged it in 1872 and again in 1877 after it was damaged by fire. Joseph Benn and Company purchased the mill in 1904. Escaping the high taxes of England, Joseph Benn and Company made a sizable investment into the construction of a new mill, mill housing and a social club. Also constructed in 1911 was the Whitehall Building. That structure housed an auditorium, shops and housing units for mill overseers. The post office that was located at 2 Greystone Avenue was relocated to the Whitehall Building in 1912 and continued in operation at that site until August 31, 1955. About one thousand employees were recruited from England, and the mill village began full operations. In 1904, the mill company also built the Greystone Primitive Methodist Church in response to the demand for a local place of worship. Soon after the war, a memorial to World War I soldiers was dedicated and was later expanded to honor World War II veterans as well.

The Second North Providence Heritage Walking Tour

Heritage Stop 1
Rhode Island Dental Surgery and Implant Center Building
Original Site of the Milk Bottle
460 Smithfield Road

The first stop of the second tour begins in a very nondescript way. A relatively new building adorns the corner of Mineral Spring Avenue and Smithfield Road. It's not what you might think of as a very historic spot. But

The unique "Milk Bottle" building was moved to Lincoln, with plans to open a creamery in it, but legal problems have prevented it from being used. Today, the building is decaying from lack of maintenance. *Photo by author.*

speculation has it that one of the oddest architectural designs in all of Rhode Island was built right here on this site. Built in the shape of a milk bottle, this structure was erected sometime around 1920. It was eventually moved to Lincoln and today is visible on Route 146, where it sits decaying. Apparently, zoning and land use issues prevent the building from being renovated and used as an ice cream stand (the reason why it was moved to the highway location many years ago).

Continue along Smithfield Road to the next building, Dr. Angelo Bigelli's office.

Heritage Stop 2
Dr. Angelo Bigelli's Office
Governor John Notte House
464 Smithfield Road

John Anthony Notte Jr. was born in Providence, Rhode Island, on May 3, 1909, to John Anthony and Eva Theresa (Rodina) Notte. He lived in North Providence for the last forty-five years of his life. A 1931 graduate

Walking Tours of the Villages of Lymansville, Allendale, Centredale and Fruit Hill

When Governor John Notte Jr. lived in this home with his family, it included a farmer's porch in the front that was removed when the lot was rezoned for commercial use. *Photo by author.*

of Providence College, he attended Cornell University from 1931 to 1932 and graduated from Boston University Law School in 1935. He set up his law practice in North Providence and served as the town solicitor in 1937. He joined the navy during World War II and rose to the rank of lieutenant. In 1948, he was appointed to the staff of Senator Theodore F. Green, a position he held until 1956 when he resigned to run for secretary of state. Notte held that post for two years.

In 1958, he successfully sought the office of lieutenant governor and, in 1960, served as a delegate to the Democratic National Convention. In 1961, he became governor of Rhode Island. During his term, he established the first family court and instituted the Rhode Island primary election structure. Notte lost his bid for reelection to John Chafee primarily because of his support of the income tax. He was the first Democrat to seek the office without the support of organized labor. In 1967, he entered the race for the U.S. House of Representatives but lost in the primary. He died of heart failure on March 7, 1983, leaving behind wife Marie J. (Huerth) Notte; son John III, a prominent Providence attorney; and daughter Joyce. He is buried at St. Francis Cemetery in Pawtucket.

Continue along Smithfield Road, bearing left at the fork. Continue down the hill for three-fourths of a mile to the Captain Stephen Olney House.

Heritage Stop 3
Captain Stephen Olney House
138 Smithfield Road

Stephen Olney was born in October 1755 in North Providence. At the age of nineteen, Stephen became a private in the North Providence Rangers, a chartered military company. On March 30, 1775, Stephen married Dorcas Smith and in May entered the Revolutionary army with Hitchcock's Fourteenth Continentals as an ensign under the command of Captain John Angell. By January 1776, he had advanced to the position of lieutenant in Captain Coggeshall Olney's company. Stephen became a captain in the Second Rhode Island Regiment in February 1777, and in 1781, he was given command of the Light Infantry Company. Captain Olney participated in the Battles of Long Island, White Plains, Brandywine, Germantown and Monmouth. He was in the Jersey retreat and was wounded at Springfield. Late in the war, he was detached to join Lafayette and served with him at Yorktown, where he was active in the capture of a British redoubt. There he received several bayonet wounds.

Captain Stephen Olney enjoyed living in this house and working his family farm. The reluctant hero is buried in the family cemetery located behind the house to the right. *Photo by author.*

Walking Tours of the Villages of Lymansville, Allendale, Centredale and Fruit Hill

Marquis de Lafayette, after learning of Olney's wounds in the war, was so moved that when they met later, Lafayette shed tears of emotion. Their friendship endured, and when Lafayette visited Rhode Island after the war, he asked to see Stephen Olney. Stephen built this two-and-a-half-story home north of his birthplace in the year 1806.

Upon his retirement from the military, Stephen Olney represented North Providence in the state legislature for twenty years. He also served as president of the town council and held a number of other town offices. Stephen died on November 23, 1832, and is buried with his wife, father, mother and other family members in the Olney family cemetery, located behind his home to the east in the Stephen Olney Park.

Across the street and three houses east of the Stephen Olney House is the Joseph Smith House.

Heritage Stop 4
Joseph Smith House
109 Smithfield Road

The stone end on the left side of this house is the only structure surviving from the King Philip's War of 1676. A combination of several Indian tribes, while rebelling against their treatment by the early settlers, burned everything in their wake until they were finally defeated in Massachusetts. *Photo by author.*

A stone-ender house was built on this site before King Philip's War, but it was destroyed by fire during that war in 1676. All that remained of the original house was the stone chimney. Shortly thereafter, a new, smaller house was built with stone utilizing that same chimney. The brick on the side of the house demarcates the addition. The current Joseph Smith House was built in 1705, making it the town's oldest existing home and the only surviving stone-ender home in North Providence. Joseph "the Weaver" was the grandson of John "the Miller" Smith, one of Rhode Island's earliest settlers. The home was greatly enlarged at the beginning of the nineteenth century. The newer part is to the right of the front door, and the plastered chimney on the right has been raised to match the new building height. In 1937, a Providence lawyer, who was a descendant of a former owner of the Greystone Mills, purchased the house. The home is still privately owned and was added to the National Register of Historic Places in 1978.

Reverse direction and walk up Smithfield Road (uphill) half a mile to the intersection of Colonial Road. Across the street is the rear entrance to the North Providence High School.

Heritage Stop 5
North Providence High School
Smithfield Road (Rear Entrance)

The North Providence High School was built in 1937–38 under the Works Progress Administration, a jobs program created by the federal government during Franklin D. Roosevelt's administration to provide relief to the many

The first graduating class from the North Providence High School after its opening in 1938 included seventy-five seniors. *Photo by author.*

people left unemployed by the Great Depression. The doors opened in September 1938, with Thomas McGovern serving as its first principal. In June 1939, 75 graduating seniors received their diplomas, the first awarded by the new high school. On March 29, 1994, an arson fire destroyed a portion of the building. For almost two years, many classes were held in temporary trailers set up in the parking lot. In September 1995, the "new" high school was dedicated. Many modern features, such as sensor lights and central air conditioning, were included in the renovation. Repair and expansion costs totaled $13 million. In June 2008, 264 graduating seniors received their North Providence High School diplomas from Joseph Goho, the school's seventh and current principal.

Walk south on Colonial Drive to the intersection with High Service Avenue and turn right. On the left is Our Lady of Fatima Hospital.

Heritage Stop 6
Our Lady of Fatima Hospital
200 High Service Avenue

Although the Diocese of Providence opened the doors of the St. Joseph Hospital in Providence on April 6, 1892, it wasn't until 1954 that demand required a new 175-bed facility be opened in North Providence. Initially

The site now occupied by the hospital once served as a reservoir for the people of North Providence. *Photo by author.*

designed as a hospital for the chronically ill, it replaced the diocese's Hillsgrove chronic care facility in Warwick. Fatima became a general hospital in 1955 and was expanded in 1960 when 100 beds were added. By the end of the 1960s, the diocese decided to merge St. Joseph and Our Lady of Fatima Hospitals under a single administration and identity. Today, the hospital is a nonprofit, general acute care facility operating under the patronage of the diocese. It offers treatment in twenty-eight medical surgical specialties and has a nationally recognized care center and twenty-four-hour emergency care center. The hospital also operates a nursing school and schools of medical technology, cytotechnology and histotechnology.

Continue west on High Service Avenue, go around the bend to the right of the hospital, turn left on Fisher Street, go two-tenths of a mile to Fruit Hill Avenue and take a left. Walk one-tenth of a mile along Fruit Hill Avenue.

Heritage Stop 7
William and Ida Angell House, Ruramount
569 Fruit Hill Avenue

William Randall Angell was born in Lincoln in 1851 to William and Mary Angell. He earned his living as a carpenter building houses. In 1904, he built

Without a doubt, the 1904 estate Ruramount remains one of the stateliest Victorian homes in the town. *Photo from the 1910 North Providence–Johnston Directory.*

this home for his own family. Originally, a reservoir was located just south of the building, and fruit trees abounded in the area. The reservoir and all but two pear trees are gone. William R. Angell died in 1918 at the age of sixty-seven. The current owners, Dr. Fred and Beverly Burgess, restored the home to showcase its elegance and beauty and planted three apple trees and a peach tree. The main building and two of three secondary buildings remain in their original locations. The garage, repaired after a fire, was originally a barn, and the fourth building no longer exists. All are set back from the road on an acre of land. Beverly Burgess was a prime mover in the initiation of the town's historic district zoning ordinance, which preserves and protects the integrity of historically significant properties. (See additional sites in the Fruit Hill Area on page 118; these can be viewed between Stops 7 and 11.)

Directly across the street on the corner of Cold Spring Avenue is the next stop.

Heritage Stop 8
Robert W. and Violet E. Lister House
560 Fruit Hill Avenue

Robert W. Lister was born in Iowa on October 22, 1881, to William M. and Annie Eliza Allison. Robert's wife, Violet, was born on September 25,

The homes on Fruit Hill Avenue represent some of the finest turn-of-the-century architecture in the town. This one was built in 1916. *Photo by author.*

1882. The couple built the house in 1916 and lived there with their children: Robert, born on January 8, 1917; Stuart S., born on July 5, 1919; and William R. Lister. Robert W. Lister was employed as the secretary/treasurer at the Centredale Worsted Mill.

Cross Fruit Hill Avenue again to the houses located on the northeast and southeast corners of Randall Street.

Heritage Stop 9
Angell Houses

William R. Angell House
557 Fruit Hill Avenue

William R. Angell also owned the lot adjacent to his home at 569 Fruit Hill Avenue. The house on this lot was built in 1908, presumably for one of his children. Upon his death on April 25, 1918, he was survived by his wife, Ida, and two children, Ida M. (Angell) Weston and Daniel Angell. It is presumed that Ida Weston lived in this home.

William R. Angell built this home for his family in 1908. *Photo by author.*

William R. Angell built this house for his son, Daniel, in1906. Records indicate that Daniel suffered a mental deficiency that caused his family much consternation. *Photo by author.*

Daniel B. Angell House
553 Fruit Hill Avenue

This home was built in 1906, presumably for Daniel, the only son of William Angell. William's last will and testament indicates that Daniel had some type of mental or emotional problem, as it leaves one-third of the estate in trust for Daniel to be paid to him "if his condition is such that" it is advisable in the opinion of the trustees (William's wife and daughter). Otherwise, the funds were to be used to "obtain the care and medical attention his present condition renders necessary." Were Daniel to be cured and his mind and intellect become such that his physicians confirm that he is not suffering from a form of insanity and is competent and able to manage and control his affairs, the trust would have turned over to Daniel without reserve.

Heritage Stop 10
William S. Allison House
551 Fruit Hill Avenue

According to the records for the town of North Providence, William Allison was born to William F. and Mary Allison on May 3, 1868. The place of

William S. Allison, the original owner of this home, served his country proudly in several key battles of the Civil War. *Photo by author.*

his birth is listed as Scituate, Rhode Island. Mary had been born in North Providence but moved to Scituate upon her marriage to William F. William S. Allison's wife, Carrie, was born on April 25, 1881. The couple built this house in Fruit Hill in 1897. William F. Allison served the Union army in the Civil War and was a veteran of Gettysburg, Cold Harbor, Bull Run and other historic Civil War battles. He died of arteriosclerosis at this home on May 5, 1925, at the age of ninety-one.

Continue down Fruit Hill Avenue four-tenths of a mile to the intersection with Smith Street, to the last house on the right.

Heritage Stop 11
Fruit Hill Apartments
1621 Smith Street

Stanton Beldon was the proprietor of the Fruit Hill Classical Institute, a highly esteemed school operated at this location. Beldon also lived here. On February 25, 1840, Beldon was appointed postmaster, and this site also served as the town's first post office. The post office remained here until July 18, 1849, when it was moved to Centredale. In 1873, the building that housed the school and post

The prestigious Fruit Hill Classical Institute once occupied this site in the same neighborhood that Mary Ann Angell Young passed her time and helped work her father's farm. *Photo by author.*

office was destroyed by fire. In 1875, Beldon erected this Victorian apartment house on the site of the former institute. The air in this part of Fruit Hill was believed to contain healing qualities, making this area a resort destination for people from Providence and surrounding locations. Rooms were rented out to those who sought to breathe the "clean air" for medicinal purposes.

Cross Smith Street and turn left. Bear right at the fork onto Fruit Hill Avenue and continue one-tenth of a mile.

Heritage Stop 12
St. James Episcopal Church
474 Fruit Hill Avenue

North Providence has a rich religious history. The Baptist meetinghouse was originally located on Smithfield Road about 1767 under the auspices of Reverend Ezekiel Angell. Upon his death in 1782, Rufus Tefft succeeded him. The church was moved to its current location in 1818 and was established as the second church in North Providence. The current building was erected in 1879.

St. James Episcopal
Church was
established in 1767
but didn't erect this
building until 1879.
Photo by author.

Cross Fruit Hill Avenue and walk about two-tenths of a mile in a southerly direction to the corner of Olney Avenue just before the Civil War memorial.

Heritage Stop 13
Stephen Whipple House, Homestead Farm
157 Olney Avenue

Stephen Whipple, a shoemaker born on July 24, 1735, bought the land at the corner of Fruit Hill Avenue and Olney Avenue from his father, Benjamin, so he could begin farming. He subsequently purchased the adjoining three-fourths of an acre from Ezra Olney. This home was built in 1767 on that parcel. He lived here with his wife, Zilpha, until the property was sold to Stephen's cousin, Jabez Whipple. Jabez was living in this home when he left his family to take up service for the colonists in the American Revolution.

Stephen Whipple
built his home here
in 1767, making this
one of the oldest
surviving structures
in North Providence.
Photo by author.

The house was sold several times, and in 1822, it was purchased by William Angell. Subsequent owners include other members of the Angell family, the Newton family and current occupants William M. Woodward and Joseph Handly.

Continue one-tenth of a mile to 119 Olney Avenue.

Heritage Stop 14
Edward Whales Olney House
119 Olney Avenue

In 1861, Ira Olney sold this house and a large parcel of land to his mother, who in turn sold to her son, Edward Wales Olney, in 1862. Edward, a real estate broker and town moderator, was born on November 11, 1822, and died on February 17, 1908. Ira's house is around the corner at 59 Homewood Avenue. All of the land in Fruit Hill was at one time owned by Ezra Olney, Ira's grandfather. Today this home is owned by Town Historian Thomas Greene and his wife, Barbara, coauthors of *Images of America: North Providence*, volumes 1 and 2.

This 1861 house was once occupied by Edward Wales Olney, a North Providence town moderator. *Photo by author.*

Heritage Stop 15
Frederick Whipple House
10 Olney Avenue

Frederick Whipple was born in Providence on July 2, 1875, the only child of George Edward and Mary Jane (Gardiner) Whipple. The house shown here was built in 1895. Frederick Whipple purchased the property from the widow Alice Hedley for $100 on February 26, 1896. On February 2, 1909, Whipple married Alice Greene, who was born on March 4, 1874. The original barn built for this house was moved to a street and is now a residential home. Today, the home is hardly recognizable from this photograph. The wraparound porch has been removed, as has the second-story porch. The latter has been replaced with an extended dormer and a picture window. The entire house is now wrapped in a beige vinyl siding and has an exposed red brick foundation.

Reverse direction and follow Olney Avenue to the intersection with Fruit Hill Avenue.

This 1895 home was purchased for a mere $100 in 1896. Today, the wraparound farmer's porch that once graced the front is no longer part of the house. *Photo from the 1910 North Providence–Johnston Directory.*

Walking Tours of the Villages of Lymansville, Allendale, Centredale and Fruit Hill

Heritage Stop 16
Soldiers and Sailors Monument
Fruit Hill Avenue

This Civil War monument was unveiled on Memorial Day, May 30, 1904, thanks to the generosity of benefactor and state senator Daniel Wanton

Above: This monument to the deceased soldiers and sailors from North Providence was one of the many contributions made to North Providence by Daniel Wanton Lyman and his family. *Author's collection.*

Right: Daniel Wanton Lyman, grandson of Lymansville's founder, was a wealthy philanthropist whose untimely death at the age of forty-two shook the town. *Author's collection.*

Lyman, who had an immense interest in the state militia. The grandson of Daniel Lyman and Governor Elisha Dyer, Daniel Wanton Lyman served in the Civil War under Major General Charles Robbins, as a major and aide-de-camp, from 1863 to 1864. A philanthropist who died at age forty-two, D.W. Lyman left money to many charities, including $5,000 for the erection of this monument. The inscription on the right reads: "Erected in honor of the soldiers and sailors enlisting from the town of North Providence who fell or died in the Civil War—Given by—Daniel Wanton Lyman." The sculptor was Alice Ruggles Kitson, who was assisted by Lillian R. Parrott and Annie E. Ogden.

Continue in a southerly direction down the easterly side of Fruit Hill to 399 Fruit Hill Avenue.

Heritage Stop 17
William H. Angell House
Franciscan Missionaries of Mary
385 Fruit Hill Avenue

William Angell built this house in 1876. It is now the property of the Franciscan Missionaries of Mary. *Photo by author.*

Walking Tours of the Villages of Lymansville, Allendale, Centredale and Fruit Hill

The William Angell House (identified as the Byron Angell House in Thomas and Barbara Greene's book) was built in 1876. William H. Angell, the son of William W. Angell, was a trial justice for North Providence for twenty years and also served in the Rhode Island Senate. His son, Byron, was born in North Providence in 1856 and married Emily Ide of Glocester in 1882 at the age of twenty-six. The couple had two sons and one daughter. In 1921, the house was sold to the Franciscan Missionaries of Mary, who still own it today. The property abuts several beautiful and peaceful acres, still owned by the Franciscans, and includes a grotto that was featured on a postcard at the turn of the nineteenth century.

Cross Fruit Hill Avenue and continue in a southerly direction to the VFW Post at 354 Fruit Hill Avenue.

Heritage Stop 18
Lymansville Memorial Post No. 10011, VFW
354 Fruit Hill Avenue

This 1879 building housed the Fruit Hill School. The building was used continuously as a schoolhouse until 1930. The first known schoolhouse in town was built in about 1768 where the Civil War statue now stands. Stephen

The VFW Hall building served as Fruit Hill's schoolhouse from 1879 to 1930. *Photo by author.*

DeBlois served as that school's master between 1791 and 1795. By 1799, the building was gone from that site. Another schoolhouse used by Fruit Hill residents was located on the corner of Mount Pleasant Avenue and Elmcrest Avenue, an area that at the time was part of North Providence. That area is now part of the city of Providence, and the schoolhouse building has been converted into a private residence. The house was later relocated to 28 Olney Avenue and is now used as a private residence.

This stop concludes the second North Providence Heritage Tour.

ADDITIONAL STOPS ON THE SECOND TOUR

Between Stops 7 and 11, there are many more houses worthy of note.

The George Lamberton House (1364 Smith Street): The current site of the Maggiacomo Insurance Agency was built in 1898. Lamberton, who was in the real estate business, lived in the house until his death in 1922.

The Samuel J. Lamberton House (1358 Smith Street): This building is currently occupied by Dr. Donald V. Fargnoli, who located his office at this site after purchasing the property in 1984. The Victorian-style home was built on this property circa 1898. Dr. Fargnoli added the additional turrets on the east side of the house when he expanded the building around the turn of the twentieth century.

The William Dracup House (1636 Smith Street): Dracup and his partners James Lister Jr. and William Mackie purchased the Centredale Worsted Mills in 1891 following one of several fires that damaged the complex. They produced worsted yarn. In 1899, Dracup was appointed to the St. Alban's Church building committee along with Frank C. Angell. He built the house at 1336 Smith Street in 1904.

The Ira Olney House (59 Homewood Avenue): This home was built in 1861 on land given to Ira Olney by his father, Cyrus, who lived in a smaller house on this site. Ezra Olney, Ira's grandfather, was the predominant landowner in Fruit Hill.

BIBLIOGRAPHY

BOOKS

Angell, Frank C. *Annals of Centredale in the Town of North Providence, Rhode Island: Its Past and Present, 1636–1909*. Salem, MA: Higginson Book Company, 1909.

Boucher, Susan Marie. *The History of Pawtucket, 1635–1976*. Hartford: Connecticut Printers Inc., 1976.

Greene, Thomas, and Barbara Greene. *Images of America: North Providence*. Volume 1. Dover, NH: Arcadia Publishing, 1996.

———. *Images of America: North Providence*. Volume 2. Dover, NH: Arcadia Publishing, 1997.

Haley, John Williams. *History of Pawtucket, Central Falls, Lincoln and Cumberland, Rhode Island, 1936*. N.p.: Lower Blackstone River Valley District Committee of the Rhode Island and Providence Plantations Tercentenary Committee, Inc., 1937.

———. *The Old Stone Bank History of Rhode Island*. Providence, RI: Providence Institutions for Savings, 1929.

———. *The Old Stone Bank History of Rhode Island*. Volume 4. Providence, RI: Providence Institutions for Savings, 1944.

———. *The Old Stone Bank History of Rhode Island*. Volume 3. Providence, RI: Providence Institutions for Savings, 1939.

———. *The Old Stone Bank History of Rhode Island*. Volume 2. Providence, RI: Providence Institutions for Savings, 1931.

Jessee, Dean C. *Brigham Young's Family*. Part I, *1824–1845*. The Mormon Church Historical Department. Utah: 1978.

Leavitt, Sarah, of Slater Mill Historic Site. *Images of America: Slater Mill.* Dover, NH: Arcadia Publishing, 1997.

Middlekauf, Robert. *The Glorious Cause: The American Revolution, 1763–1789.* New York: Oxford University Press, 1982.

Nevitt, Trevor, Colonel, and Grace P. Hayes. *The Military History of the Revolutionary War Naval Battles.* New York: Franklin Watts, Inc., 1970.

Sampson, Amory C. *Daniel Wanton Lyman, 1844–1886: An Appreciation.* Providence, RI: Standard Printing Company, 1913.

St. Lawrence Church. *St. Lawrence Church, Centredale, RI, 1907–1982.* Hackensack, NJ: Custombook, Inc., 1982.

White, George S. *Memoir of Samuel Slater, the Father of American Manufactures.* 2nd ed. Philadelphia, PA: self-published, 1836.

E-BOOKS

Brigham Young's Death. Chapter 22. N.p.: Globusz Publishing, 2001–2012.

INTERVIEWS BY AUTHOR

Gertrude Baron, daughter of early 1900s Centredale postmaster Charles Baron and niece of Centredale's only postmistress, Emma Baron, 2009.

Jeffrey Gibbons, grandson of Senator Frank Sgambato, North Providence, Rhode Island, May 2009.

Thomas Greene, North Providence town historian, North Providence, Rhode Island, May 2009.

MAGAZINES

Home magazine 9, issue 3. "Great Writing on History: Father of Our Factory System" (1958). American Heritage Collections.

MISCELLANEOUS

Frank C. Angell Memorial Town Hall dedication program, September 10, 1931.

Incorporation of the Town, June 24, 1865. Pawtucket, RI: Robert Sherman, Printer, 1865.

"Report of the Celebration at Pawtucket, North Providence, of the One Hundredth Anniversary of the Inaugural Address of Frederic C. Sayles, Mayor of the City of Pawtucket," delivered January 4, 1886.

Rhode Island: A Guide to the Smallest State, High Roads and Low Roads from Taunton to Putnam. State of Rhode Island, 1865.

Rivard, Paul E. "Samuel Slater: Father of American Manufactures." Slater Mill Historic Site, 1974.

Williams, Roger. "Rhode Island's Tercentenary, 1636–1936, A Report by the Rhode Island Tercentenary Commission on the Celebration of the Three Hundredth Anniversary of the Settlement of the State of Rhode Island and Providence Plantations in 1636." Commissioned, written, and printed/published by the State of Rhode Island, 1937.

NEWSPAPERS

Kohn, Stephen M. "The Whistle-Blowers of 1777." *New York Times*, June 12, 2011.

New York Times. "Brigham Young's First Wife: Her Recent Death in Salt Lake City—Mormon Estimates of Her Sacrifices and Her Worth." July 5, 1882.

Wadley, Carma. "Pioneer Personas: Couple Enjoys Bringing Brigham Young, Mary Ann Angell Young to Life." *Deseret News*, July 24, 2011.

Washington Post. "Earliest of Sea Fighters: The First Captain Ever Appointed in the US Navy (A Short Biography of Esek Hopkins)." April 14, 1907.

PAPERS AND MANUSCRIPTS

Esek Hopkins Papers, 1755–86. Rhode Island Historical Society, Manuscripts Division. Elizabeth Delmage, processor, August 2005.

VIDEOS

Pistachio-Bessette, Judith. *Lymansville: 200 Years of Immigrant and Textile History.* 2008.

Websites

Bellis, Mary. http://www.ancestry.comMemoirs of the Wilkinson Family in America 1869—Third Generation, Connecticut. freepages.misc. rootsweb.ancestry.com/bbunce77/wilkinson004.html.

Gaspee Virtual Archives. "Admiral Esek Hopkins (1718–1802): An Historical Sketch of the Town of Scituate, RI, Part 2." www.gaspee.org.

Hickman, Kennedy. "American Revolution: John Paul Jones." militaryhistory.about.com/od/naval/p/johnpauljones.htm, 2012.

———. "The Textile Revolution: Samuel Slater Builds Spinning Mill." inventors.about.com/od/sstartinventors/a/Samuel_Slater.htm.

Holbrook Family Organization. "Caroline Frances Angell Davis Holbrook, 1825–1908: A Sketch of the Life and Experiences of Caroline Frances Angell Davis Holbrook." http://www.boap.org/LDS/Early-Saints/CAngell.html.

Jensen, Rex G. "Brigham Young: Second President of the Church." Chapter 2 in *Presidents of the Church Student Manual*, 2008. www.lds.org.

———. "The Indomitable Mary Ann." *Liahona* (April 1997). www.lds.org. Official Website of the Church of Jesus Christ of Latter-Day Saints.

Lenfestey, James P. "Brigham Young's Rebellious Wife." History Channel Club, July 6, 2009. www.thehistorychannelclub.com.

Lienhard, John H. "No. 384: Samuel Slater," 1988–97. http://www.uh.edu/engines/epi384.htm.

Naval Historical Center. Department of the Navy, Washington, D.C. www.history.navy.mil/photo/pers-us/uspers-h/e-hopk-c.htm.

Samuel Slater. "Samuel Slater—Hero or Traitor?" Maypole Promotions, 2005. www.samuelslater.co.uk/history.htm.

Tanner, Sandra. "One of My Family's Best Kept Secrets." Holbrook Family Organization. www.boap.org/LDS/Early-Saints/CAngell.html.

Van Wagoner, Richard S. "The Prophet's Family Circle—His Wives and Children," Chapter 30. Think Link. www.think-link.org.

———. "What Mormon Women Felt About Polygamy: A History." Chapter 9. Think Link. www.think-link.org.

Wikipedia. "Battle of Block Island." http://en.wikipedia.org/wiki/Battle_of_Block_Island. Last modified on December 17, 2011.

———. "Mary Ann Angell Young." http://en.wikipedia.org/wiki/Mary_Ann_Angell_Young. Find-A-Grave Memorial #183989, February 2, 2000. Created by S.M. Smith.

————. "Samuel Slater." http://en.wikipedia.org/wiki/Samuel_Slater. Last modified on April 18, 2012.

Woonsocket Connection. "Samuel Slater: Father of the American Industrial Revolution, Child Labor." www.woonsocket.org/slatervillagelife.html.

————. "Samuel Slater: Father of the American Industrial Revolution, Rhode Island's Mill Villages." www.woonsocket.org/slatervillagelife.html.

————. "Samuel Slater: Father of the American Industrial Revolution, Samuel Slater." www.woonsocket.org/slatervillagelife.html.

INDEX

ABOUT THE AUTHOR

P aul F. Caranci is a third-generation resident of Centredale and has been a student of municipal and state history for many years. Together with his wife, Margie, he founded the Municipal Heritage Group in 2009. Paul has served as Rhode Island's deputy secretary of state to the Honorable A. Ralph Mollis since 2007 and served on the North Providence Town Council from 1994 to 2010. He has a BA in political science from Providence College and currently attends Roger Williams University, earning a master's degree in public administration. He and Margie have two children (Heather and Matthew) and four grandchildren (Matthew Jr., Jacob, Vincent and Casey). Matthew and his three children are the fourth and fifth generations of the Caranci family to live in Centredale.

Visit us at
www.historypress.net

It was a sanctuary for religious dissenters and the birthplace of industrial giants.

In 1765, settlers to the west of Providence petitioned to form their own township. Their prayers were answered, and North Providence, Rhode Island, was born. While it sheltered religious dissenters, North Providence was also the sparking point of the Industrial Revolution—native sons and industrialists Samuel Slater and Zachariah Allen reinvented the cotton industry and altered the course of the nation. In this history of North Providence, author Paul F. Caranci celebrates the town's colorful characters and provides walking tours for the villages of Lymansville, Allendale, Centredale and Fruit Hill. Learn how North Providence native Stephen Olney became a Revolutionary War hero when he pulled an injured James Monroe from the battlefield and how Frank C. Angell became a spokesman for Centredale. Caranci reveals the unique history of North Providence and the people who shaped it.

$19.99

ISBN 978-1-60949-718-7

THE
History
PRESS

WWW.HISTORYPRESS.NET